MODERN LIFE
As good as it gets?

MODERN LIFE

As good as it gets?

RICHARD DOCWRA

green books

First published in the UK in 2008
by Green Books Ltd,
Foxhole, Dartington,
Totnes, Devon TQ9 6EB

ISBN 978 1 903998 97 7

Text printed on 100% recycled paper
by TJ International, Padstow, Cornwall, UK

Contents

Acknowledgements

Many people have supported me in my unusual choice of work in recent years, and it is impossible to thank them all by name. I'd like to extend my gratitude to everyone – whether friends, family, work colleagues or other contacts – who has helped me in any way over this time.

Particular thanks in the development of this book go to Inga Zeisset, Matthew Chambers, Rob Whitehead, Jeremy Singer, Adrian Docwra, Flynn Best, Andrew Thorp, Tobin Aldrich, Tim Walker, Neil Sinden (CPRE), Perry Walker (NEF) and Guy Rubin (NEF).

Many thanks also to John, Michael, Amanda and Bee at Green Books.

Dedication

To my wife, family and friends.

Introduction

We are so lucky. As individuals living in some of the richest countries in the world, we have greater material wealth than most other people on the planet, either living now or at any time in history. We have a longer life expectancy than previous generations, access to an abundance of material resources, and a wide range of opportunities.

But things are still not quite right. Our increased material wealth has not made us any happier, and some aspects of modern life in the Western world actually seem to be reducing our happiness and quality of life.

I have not written this book to moan about the state of things. I have written it because I believe we are living in an age in which there are enough resources to go round, and in which life could be good for many, many people. If life is not as good as it could be for us – the supposed 'lucky ones' in the world – we must be getting something wrong. The purpose of this book is to consider what we might be getting wrong, and what we can do about it.

One of my reasons for writing this book is that early in my adult life, I felt unsettled, confused and unsatisfied with various aspects of the modern world. After some time, I began to understand the influences behind this dissatisfaction, and was able to move towards the life that was right for me. My journey to this point took several years and was often a difficult and isolating experience, so I would like to help other people who might be on the same journey to complete it more quickly and easily than I did. I would also like to encourage those who haven't thought about these things much to do so – as it could improve their lives and those of countless others. I am not trying to be puritanical, a Luddite or a killjoy. I've got no religious axe to grind. I just want to see everyone leading lives in which we can all flourish.

A central aim of this book is to consider how particular aspects of the modern world can have a negative effect on our lives in the West. Given my own experience, the book aims not only to consider how the modern world can affect us as individuals, but also to articulate the profound way in which certain aspects of modern life can change the way we think, feel and approach our lives.

To understand the importance of certain global issues, and in particular, why seemingly benign things such as a particular economic philosophy or a phenomenon such as advertising are worth worrying about, we need to recognise the massive effects of the external world on our subjective world-views and experiences as individuals. I don't believe that these arguments have yet been made powerfully enough, and I want to explore them in this book.

The book is divided into three parts: the problems, the causes and the solutions. Part One will look at a number of aspects of day-to-day life that are harmful to our well-being – including the fast and pressurised lifestyles we lead, the influence of consumerism, our lack of connection to local communities and the lack of perspective we have in our lives.

There are many other areas of modern life I could have chosen, but I have selected these eight areas because they are varied and, in some cases, have not been adequately explored in the mainstream media. Moreover, some of the problems, although they initially appear to be quite different, actually share some common features.

Part Two considers some of the causes of the problems in Part One. Many share some important common causes, including the particular brand of economic thinking that dominates modern society and our lack of the mental tools necessary to live happily and get the most out of life. Not only are these significant influences on the problems in our own lives, but they (particularly the dominant brand of economic thinking) are also major contributors to some of the biggest problems we face on a global level, such as the environment and extreme poverty. Part Two therefore concludes that we must do something urgently about these overarching causes in order to make life better – not only for ourselves in the West, but for everyone, and to protect our planet's future.

In Part Three, I explore what can be done to address these issues. It is divided into two sections. Chapter 10 explores the changes that could be made to our society as a whole, discussing the need for a 'new economics' that refocuses the aim of society away from the never-ending pursuit of material wealth to maximising the well-being of people within the limits of the planet. It also recommends that everyone should be taught to develop a particular range of thinking skills, ranging from the 'art of living' to 'intellectual independence', which will help us to navigate our way effectively through the modern world and to live the lives we want.

Chapter 11 presents a range of steps we can each take individually. These include a 'Three-Step Programme' to help people start to develop the mental skills to live a happier and more self-determined life. It also includes a number of specific recommendations for actions to take on each of the areas discussed in Part One, from shopping locally to support your local economy, through to breaking down social barriers between you and the people around you.

At the end of the book, further reading and web links are recommended to help you find out more about some of the issues raised and to begin to take action on these matters.

This book cannot, of course, cover every problem in modern life. Moreover, even within the areas I have chosen to cover, I can only provide a broad overview, and some of the theoretical ideas are not discussed in detail. There are some topics that I take more time to discuss than others (for example, the assumptions behind the dominant brand of economic thinking, and the description of the various thinking skills I am recommending); this is because I feel there is a need to 'unpack' them more, either because they are complex ideas that are not often stripped down to their most basic principles, or because they are topics that may be unfamiliar.

My ultimate aim throughout the book is simply to present a way of achieving a better world for everyone. I hope it is a vision that you will find attractive and worth working towards.

Part One

The Problems

Chapter 1

'Our lives are too rushed'

"How are you?" "Oh, busy as ever."

Millions of conversations begin with this kind of exchange every day. Our lives may well be very busy, but why should we choose this specific word to summarise the state of our lives to people we've not seen recently? Is it because we spend most of our time living life at a frenetic pace and trying to juggle various activities and responsibilities? Or is it because we have got used to using it as a phrase – as a basic description of our lives as we see them? Or do we sometimes use it falsely because we feel it is rather shameful not to be busy?

This chapter will consider why we live in such a fast, rushed and busy culture, and some of the disadvantages of living in this way.

The pace of modern life

In the West, our lives are more rushed than they have ever been, and many people do not enjoy a reasonable work/life balance. Despite the fact that over the last 150 years annual working time in the industrialised countries has fallen steadily, from around 3,000 hours to between 1,400 and 1,800 hours,[1] there was a point in the 1980s at which this decline stopped. The average working week in the UK is now 43.2 hours, which is among the highest in Europe.[2]

Just over 22% of UK men who work full-time work over 48 hours a week (classed by the Working Time Regulations as 'long hours') – this is the highest in Europe, and compares with an average of 11% across the other EU member states. Beyond Europe it is even worse – a quarter of men in the US work over 48 hours a week, as do around one third of men in Australia and 36% of men in Japan.[3]

Some employers and governments have begun to take the issue of work/life balance seriously, although it could be argued that they have focused on increasing the 'flexibility' of working hours rather than reducing them.

The number of working hours is not the only indicator of how rushed work makes us feel however, as there is also the question of the intensity of our work. This seems to have increased in recent years as, with the help of technologies, it becomes possible to perform many tasks simultaneously.[4] Technology enables us to perform tasks with greater speed and intensity, and the competitive nature of the economy demands that we pass these gains on to the marketplace, making our roles increasingly pressurised.

Most of us have to work, and for many people having an appropriate job is an important part of their sense of identity and fulfilment in life. But work is just one of many aspects of our lives, and for many people it plays far too dominant a role, with their work circumstances controlling other areas of their lives, such as family time and social life.

It is not only the time spent at work that takes time away from other priorities in our lives. The average worker in the UK spends 139 hours a year travelling to and from work[5] – time which could potentially be spent on other things.

Our work/life balance is not the only problem. Even when we have some control over our work time, many people are constantly hopping from one activity to another outside work, trying to balance a range of commitments and interests in their leisure time – from family life to shopping through to socialising. Not only are we often time-pressured, but even when we're not we seem to want to cram as much as possible into our lives, making them a sprint through a series of activities rather than a walk in which we enjoy the view and allow life to unfold in front of us. Leisure, as well as work, has become more intensive.

One of the factors shaping the way we approach our lives is the importance of 'speed' within our Western culture – fast food, speed dating, 24 hour news – life 'in the fast lane' seems to be something to aspire to. Labour-saving devices continue to be invented in order to save us time. But why do we see time as something that has to be saved, or something into which we need to cram as much activity as possible? Behind this thinking seems to lie a particular view of what life is about, and in the next section we will consider what this view might be for many people.

A concept linked to the notions of 'rushing' and 'being busy' is that of 'doing'. Just as we like to feel we are busy, many of us also like to show others that we have been doing lots of different activities. A conversation to catch up with someone you've not spoken to for a while can become a list of exciting things that each of you has done recently – rather like ticking off a range of items on a list. If you happen to have adopted a way of life that is not filled with a constant range of new activities, then conversations like this can be more difficult. "So, what have you been up to?" "Oh, I've read some good books, seen some friends, pottered in the garden."

Why are we so rushed?

Influences on our current attitudes towards time can be traced back to early Christianity, which not only warned against laziness but also developed a regimented, disciplined attitude towards time – for example, within the codes for monastic living set down within the Rule of Saint Benedict, which was influential in the Church in the Middle Ages. As the power and influence of the Church spread, so did its values.

Perhaps the most obvious influence on our modern attitude towards time was the Industrial Revolution and the advent of industrial capitalism. At this point, industrialists began to see a worker's time in the workplace as a resource to be managed – efficient use of this resource resulted in increased productivity and therefore larger profits. Benjamin Franklin's dictum – 'time is money' – became a driving philosophy.

The growth and dominance of the capitalist system since the Industrial Revolution has meant that its philosophy of time has continued to dominate western society to the present day. Time has become "a currency that we can spend or save, a resource, an economic variable".[6] This philosophy of time has seeped into our attitudes and values in various ways – not simply with the idea that 'time is money', but also in our obsession with speed and efficiency, the idea that non-economically productive work like childcare is less valuable than economically productive work, and the idea that laziness is bad and being busy is good. Capitalism seems to have exacerbated the puritanical view of time we inherited from Christianity.

Advances in technology and communications during the twentieth and twenty-first centuries have enabled us to achieve ever faster responses to the demands of capitalism, but at the same time have pushed our obsession with speed and efficiency to ever greater heights.

Our concept of time has therefore changed over the years according to our social, cultural and economic circumstances – our view of time comes down to what is valued in a society at a particular point. Our modern view of time seems to have become embedded in our culture to such an extent that we do not realise that it carries particular values with it.

Before the imposition of our strict, mechanised and morally loaded view of time, things were very different. We had not ascribed any arbitrary, puritanical values to our use of time, and our relationship with it was tied to nature. Tom Hodgkinson, editor of *The Idler* magazine, describes it thus:

> "Joyful chaos, working in tune with the seasons, telling the time by the sun, variety, change, self-direction; all this was replaced with a brutal, standardised work culture, the effects of which we are still suffering from today." [7]

Our adoption of the idea of time as a currency is not just confined to the workplace. It has extended into the way we view time generally. We see it as something that needs to be 'spent wisely', and we put pressure on ourselves to do this. A good example of this is in our desire to cram as much as possible into our daily lives. Being busy is seen as an admirable trait and a sign of social status, as one is being a 'productive' person. So not only do we spend our working lives in a pressurised relationship with time trying to be 'productive' for our employers, but we also seem to pressurise ourselves to maximise our 'productivity' in our social lives!

A glance at the history of our attitude towards time also seems to suggest a reason for the modern tendency to see social life as a range of activities to be ticked off a list. Perhaps we have come to regard social activities as 'commodities' that we 'consume', and we feel the need to consume more of them, just as we do with the latest products and services. The idea of persevering with an existing activity seems to run contrary to our modern desire for novelty.

What's wrong with being rushed?

Being rushed can damage our health

Attempting to keep up an intensive pace of life can take its toll on both our physical and mental health. We can feel pressurised and stressed, and not take time to care for ourselves properly – for example, if we often grab a snack to eat 'on the run' or buy convenience food, instead of following a healthy diet.

The experience of trying to cram too much into our lives may not be the only thing that can have a negative effect on our health. The prioritisation of speed and 'busy-ness' can also create a form of status anxiety – the feeling that if we aren't frantically busy then we aren't valued members of society.

Rushing is unsustainable

Our current obsession with speed is damaging our prospects of having a good quality of life (not to mention survival) in the future, partially because "the faster we live, the faster we consume the planet's finite resources and trash the natural systems on which we depend,"[8] and also because our obsession with speed leads us to focus on the short-term, rather than on adopting the long-term vision and self-regulation that will be necessary to secure a sustainable future.

We're not in control of our lives when we're rushed

Once we get onto the treadmill of rushing, we can be in danger of relinquishing control of our lives, as we are swept away by the overwhelming, endless flow of demands that we and society place on ourselves. To quote James Goodman and Britt Jorgensen in *About Time*:

> "Much of the stress that we feel in our everyday lives stems from a feeling that our time is not really our time. We have no control over it and, despite our best efforts, have become slaves to the unrelenting onward march."[9]

Living at high speed can also become habitual, leading us to feel that something is missing if we are not rushing all the time.

Overwork can prevent us from giving enough time to other priorities

We may be missing out on other priorities in life because of overwork. In a 2007 report, the National Centre for Social Research found that, among people working full-time, 84% of women and 82% of men would like to spend more time with their family.[10]

Most people have priorities in life other than just paid work, for what is the point of life if we are not able to give time to the things that we care about?

We might not want our lives to be this way

This culture of speed has spread from our working lives into our private lives. We can be caught in a vicious circle: we have little time to stand back and reflect on what we really want in life – to step off the treadmill, relax and consider our real priorities and goals. If we don't do this, we may not even realise that we are not living the kind of lives we really want. We also need time to be able to think creatively about what inspires and interests us, and develop new interests.

We also have little opportunity to consider how much time we should give to different areas of our lives in order to get the most out of them. And this leads us to another key point – the importance of enjoying our time.

We may be so rushed, and juggling so many activities, that we aren't fully engaged in, or enjoying, the activity we are currently doing because we are thinking about the next one. This highlights a faulty assumption at the heart of the culture of speed – the assumption that life is just a series of activities that are purchased with a currency called time, and that we should try to maximise the number of these activities. This is a one-dimensional view of time, and indeed life. There is also a dimension of quality as well as quantity to life – of appreciating the experience at a given moment. To be able to do this, we need to concentrate on the present moment, without cluttering up our minds with worries, plans and thoughts for the future.

Additionally, we might each have different views about what makes for a good quality of life, and different views about how we should balance the dimensions of quantity and quality in our lives. For example, some of us may feel that we don't have to do specific activities – or anything in particular – in order to enjoy our lives. Appreciating and enjoying the profound experience of being alive can be one of the great pleasures of life. The famous lines from 'Leisure' by W. H. Davies are pertinent:

What is this life if, full of care,
We have no time to stand and stare.[11]

We should be wary of any doctrine (whether capitalism, religion or environmentalism) that tells us that we should adopt a particular balance between quality and quantity, because such a recommendation will invariably be built on arbitrary assumptions about what is important in life. Following anything other than our own preferences is likely to be damaging to us, as we will not be living the lives we really want. Being endlessly busy may simply not be the way of life that we really want.

We don't have a choice about being rushed

There is nothing wrong with being busy *per se*. Work can be an important source of identity, purpose and fulfilment, and a busy social life outside work can be fun. A quiet life may not be to everyone's taste.

We should, however, be able to make a conscious choice about the kind of lives we want to lead, and the pace at which we want to lead them. The dominance of our speed-focused culture makes it hard for most people to see that such a choice is available to them, as the only speed available in modern mainstream society seems to be 'fast'. This has a number of effects on us besides those we have already discussed.

Firstly, it can be difficult not to be influenced by the norms of society. The dominance of the culture of speed may affect us in a negative way without us realising it. It may lead us to believe that this is the only way to live, and that if we aren't thriving in this environment, then there must be something wrong with us. It becomes difficult to see that we actually have a choice about the pace, quality and type of lives we want.

Secondly, even if we do get to the point of wanting to get off the treadmill, it can be difficult to actually do so, because the alternatives to this lifestyle can not only be difficult to identify but can also represent too much of a sacrifice and change. In this situation, the path of least resistance seems to be to carry on as we are.

One reason why getting off the treadmill seems to be such a sacrifice is that most of our life plans in the West follow a particular model of how to live. In this model, our life plans are built around the idea that we will need to be as productive as possible with our time until we retire, when we can enjoy some rest (and then gently expire, having worked ourselves into the ground for most of our lives). This has been the traditional life plan of a worker in a capitalist society for decades and is the model that accompanies our culture of speed and 'busy-ness'.

Most people under the age of 65 are therefore busily trying to build up and pay off a range of major financial commitments (including mortgages and other loans) they have made in order to stand themselves in good shape for their old age, whilst also trying to maintain a consumerist lifestyle in the meantime. The prospect of making changes in the short-term such as 'downsizing' our level of working, our range of commitments or even the speed of our lives might seem to be difficult in the face of these other long-term priorities in our lives.

But why should we delay living until we are old? And do we really need to consume as much as we currently do in order to be happy? Do we really need to earn as much, and therefore work as much, as we do? As this book will show, moving towards a different life plan that allows us to live the life we want, throughout our whole life, may not be as difficult as it seems.

Not only have our lives become too rushed, but also some of the places that are most important in helping us to relax and gain some balance in our lives are under threat. The next chapter examines this threat to our natural spaces.

Chapter 2

'Our natural spaces are under threat'

Our green, unpopulated spaces are vital to our well-being. This chapter will consider the threats to these natural spaces and the importance of preserving them. A strong argument can be made for the protection of natural spaces simply on the basis that they are important contributors to our own peace of mind and well-being, and also because preserving them should be an end in itself.

The threats to tranquillity

A report by The Campaign to Protect Rural England (CPRE) states:

> We can . . . find tranquillity in urban areas – in gardens, parks, allotments and local nature reserves. These green urban areas are a precious resource which should be safeguarded. But England's varied and beautiful countryside offers us a much wider opportunity to experience 'deep tranquillity'.[1]

Deep tranquillity is a feeling of profound peace, calm and well-being. This feeling can be brought about by certain conditions around us. The CPRE questioned members of the public to find out what they thought tranquillity consisted of,[2] and the top responses, in descending order, were:

- Seeing a natural landscape
- Hearing birdsong
- Hearing peace and quiet
- Seeing natural looking woodland
- Seeing the stars at night
- Seeing streams
- Seeing the sea
- Hearing natural sounds

We are most likely to experience this tranquillity in open, natural spaces. But these rural spaces are under threat. In the UK, space is at a premium, and we currently lose 21 square miles of countryside (an area larger than Southampton) to new development each year.[3] Green Belts – often known as the 'lungs' of cities and supposedly protected from development – are being chipped away, with around 1,000 hectares a year being lost to development.[4]

A combination of factors is contributing to the threat to our natural spaces, but the one with the most severe impact is housing development. There is clearly a need for new housing in Britain: house prices have risen to very high levels in the last decade, and there is a particular shortage of affordable housing. In 2002 only 37% of new households could afford to buy a property, as compared with 46% in the late 1980s.[5] The government has stated that it aims for at least 200,000 new homes to be built each year by 2016.[6] This additional housing will of course need to be accompanied by the infrastructure needed to support it, including shops, hospitals, schools and universities.

Housing is not the only factor, however. The new road building planned for the next few years will also reduce tranquillity, both through the roads themselves and through the effects of these roads, such as increased traffic and noise levels. Roads also establish new arteries along which other forms of development (and their associated reductions in tranquillity) can take place: for example road lighting, housing and retail outlets. Traffic levels are forecast to rise by 30% between 2000 and 2015 if current trends continue.[7]

Even apparently small changes to the natural landscape can make a difference to its tranquillity. For example, it might be argued that a road is only a strip of tarmac five metres wide, but its effects are much greater than this suggests. It carries traffic which brings noise, disrupts views, can be dangerous, and is also a barrier to a pedestrian's thoroughfare in the countryside. A landscape is therefore fundamentally changed by a road – divided by it, sliced in two by it, with tranquillity removed from both of the two resulting plots.

Once the 'slicing' process referred to above has begun on an area of land, it also becomes progressively easier for developers to argue that the resulting land is of less conservation value – thus leading to a 'slippery slope' argument for all kinds of development on unspoilt areas. This argument was illustrated by Environment Secretary David Miliband in a speech at CPRE's eightieth anniversary conference:

"St James's Park occupies 58 acres of prime real estate in Central London – with huge potential development value, worth, based on conservative estimates, £170 million, and probably much more. Conventional cost benefit analysis would justify taking a corner of St James's Park and developing it. And then taking another edge and developing that. But as each corner was sliced off, we would soon discover that a magnificent national and international asset had been eroded to a sad remnant of land – and the argument for complete development would be unstoppable." [8]

Another factor threatening tranquillity is the further expansion of the aviation industry. The Government's Aviation White Paper produced in 2003 signalled its intention to allow the expansion of airports and air travel to continue. This policy not only displays a highly questionable level of consistency with the government's pledge for Britain to "set an example to the rest of the world"[9] in confronting climate change, but also opens the door to a range of developments that further threaten rural areas and tranquillity generally. These include the expansion of airports (a second runway at Gatwick will alone require nearly 600 acres of land)[10] and increased numbers of flights (a major source of noise in both urban and rural areas).

Why the threats exist

This is just a selection of the threats to our tranquillity. The factors driving them are complex and cannot be covered in detail here, but a few examples should give an indication of the main ones:

- Housing – influences include rising population levels, a reduction in the size of households (the general trend for fewer people living in each home) and more people using the property market as an investment tool;

- Roads – a growth in car ownership and a lack of public transport alternatives to car use have contributed to the growth of roads;

- Aviation – air travel has increased through a range of influences including greater affluence, advances in technology and the subsidies and tax breaks (such as tax-free aviation fuel) that have been enjoyed by airlines.

Overarching some of these factors is the fact that the principles of sustainable development are not a sufficiently strong driving force behind our transport and planning infrastructure, and government policy on sustainable development is not sufficiently 'joined up' across different areas of policy. As car ownership goes up we build more roads to accommodate them without questioning whether we should have fewer cars.

Aside from these factors, there is also a major issue for modern humanity to resolve. Climbing population levels are putting pressure on our land resources, not just in England but throughout the world. With global population levels expected to rise from the current figure of around 6.7 billion to over 9 billion by 2050,[11] the pressures caused by this growth on a finite supply of land and natural space will be an issue for most countries in the future. One consequence of this is that there will be continuing pressure from commercial interests to develop land, as it will have a growing economic value as an increasingly scarce resource. And for these commercial interests, the land's value will be in its potential for development rather than its value as a natural space.

We will have to address the genuinely challenging question of how (and to what level) we should protect our natural spaces and tranquillity from the tide of development and human impact gradually eroding them away. Where, and how, do we draw the line?

What's wrong with the disappearance of natural tranquillity?

This section will consider the importance of natural spaces for reasons beyond the critical role they play in our survival, such as providing food, water, air and other resources.

We're losing something that we value

We appear to be destroying something that we value highly. A 2005 MORI poll for the CPRE found that 84% of people in England believe that Green Belt land should remain open and undeveloped, and that building on Green Belt land should not be allowed.[12]

We're losing something that is good for us

The peaceful natural landscape is good for both our physical and our mental well-being. Our physical health can be improved by the fresh air, peace and opportunities for exercise that natural spaces offer. The CPRE suggests that "exposure to nature has also been shown to reduce blood pressure, reduce heart attacks, increase mental performance and soothe anxiety." [13]

Exposure to the natural landscape also improves various aspects of our mental health. Evidence from the Countryside Recreation Network suggests that "nature can help us recover from pre-existing stresses or problems, have an 'immunising' effect by protecting us from future stresses and help us to concentrate and think more clearly". [14] Indeed, many people regard 'getting out into the countryside' as a way of tackling stress. Just to illustrate this, close your eyes and imagine yourself sitting in a field in the countryside – the sun is shining, a gentle breeze is stroking your face, the birds are twittering and there is peace – can you not feel yourself becoming calmer simply by imagining this scenario?

Being in the countryside also brings a sense of freedom, space and contact with nature that induces happiness. In *Walden*, Henry David Thoreau quotes a line from Krishna in the *Harivamsa*: "There are none happy in the world but beings who enjoy freely a vast horizon." [15]

We're losing something that gives us perspective

Exposure to nature seems to be a positive factor in our mental development, both as children and adults.

Visiting the countryside is an effective way to teach children about some elementary aspects of the world (for example, understanding where their food comes from), as they see these things at first hand and experience them personally. Outdoor education can also promote many other aspects of a child's development, such as working with others, developing new skills, undertaking practical conservation and influencing society. [16] A large proportion of people in the UK live in urban areas, and many children grow up with little exposure to nature.

In adulthood, exposure to the natural environment can help us to 'get away from it all', stand back from our lives and see things in perspective. In fact, it is one of the simplest and most powerful forms of perspective we can gain, reminding us of the natural reality we're actually living in when human embellishments such as buildings and roads are removed, and the fact that we are creatures ourselves. As we will see in Chapter 10, this ability to stand back and see the big picture has a range of benefits, from making us feel calmer to giving us a greater level of wisdom about our lives and how to lead them.

We're losing something that's good for local economies

Government figures suggest that rural tourism nationally supports around 380,000 jobs and contributes £13.8 billion annually to the economy.[17] Citing MORI survey data, the CPRE suggest that 49% of people visit the countryside for its tranquillity, and thus that tranquillity is responsible for almost half of the money generated by the rural tourist economy.

We're losing something of great beauty

Whilst some might argue that beauty is subjective, throughout history human beings have wondered at the beauty of their natural environment. Inspiration from this beauty and a desire to communicate it has driven some of our greatest artists, musicians and writers to produce some of humanity's most cherished creative work. And even if we cannot articulate it with quite the same majesty as the great artists, many of the rest of us have shared their appreciation of nature.

Nature is important in its own right

There is also a matter of principle at stake here. For millennia we have had the idea that nature is a resource for human beings to utilise. This assumption has held sway from early Christianity, through the Enlightenment in thinkers such as John Locke, to the present day. It is also an assumption with no foundations whatsoever. It is no less valid (although, it must be acknowledged, it is an equally arbitrary moral judgement) to argue that nature should be protected for its own sake, as a thing that transcends its value to human beings or its market value – that has value in itself.

I believe that the sensible position lies somewhere between these two views. We need the natural environment in order to survive, and as we have seen, it provides us with many other benefits. In this sense it acts as a resource for human beings. But our natural spaces are not a resource in the market-driven sense of the word – something that can have a financial value attached to it, and that can therefore be compromised or sold should something else (in the market's eyes) have a 'higher' value. We should set aside a certain proportion of our natural spaces and agree that they cannot be compromised for human interests – showing we acknowledge that they have value in their own right. Quite how much natural space we should elevate to this status is part of the 'major issue' of population discussed earlier in this chapter, which will be revisited briefly in Part Three.

The loss is irreversible

In our modern capitalist economy, once we have developed a piece of land, the chances are that it will remain developed. I am not suggesting that it is impossible to restore developed land to some form of natural beauty over time – this process has been undertaken with disused coal fields and various other areas. It is however highly unlikely that most land that has been developed will be returned to its unpopulated, natural state. This is because, as we noted earlier, as soon as land is seen simply as a resource and its use driven by the market, that land will be at the mercy of the whims of the market. And the market is only geared up to see value in nature in economic terms – not in its own right or in its contribution to human well-being. Once a natural space has been developed, there are two scenarios that are far more likely than the space being returned to its natural state. Either developers will continue to find a financially profitable use for it or they will leave it as a wasteland, because there is no financial recompense to be gained from restoring it to its natural state.

Aside from this, the loss of certain habitats to development can mean the loss of certain species forever, or it can take many years – sometimes generations – to restore them to their original state.

The loss of many natural spaces in the modern world is therefore most unlikely to be reversed, and we must therefore manage the remaining ones with extreme care.

Chapter 3

'Shopping is hell'

The modern shopping experience is depressing. The supermarket is a huge shed, the size of an aircraft hangar. Artificial lighting illuminates the aisles. Self-absorbed people push their trolleys around like robots, trying to do their shopping and get out as quickly as possible. Stressed mothers try to control screaming children. At the cash desk, you are served by a depressed-looking teenager. Queues of cars wait to get in and out of the huge car park.

In this chapter we'll look at two major aspects of the modern shopping experience: firstly the dominance of shopping malls, supermarkets and out-of-town outlets, and secondly the homogenisation and disintegration of our local high streets.

Recent changes

The experience of shopping has changed beyond recognition in the last fifty years. Where once we bought our groceries from a variety of shops in our local high street, many of us now leave our local area and buy all our goods from one place – an out-of-town supermarket.

Perhaps the most radical change has taken place over the last twenty years. A small number of leading names (including Tesco, Sainsbury's and Asda) now control a substantial proportion of the UK grocery market, with much of their expansion attributable to their development of large superstores, often more than 1,000 square metres in size. Between 1986 and 1997, the number of these superstores rose from 457 to 1,102.[1] By 2003, the leading retailers were operating 5,413 spaces of 25,000 square feet or more.[2]

As well as large supermarkets, we have seen the arrival of another new phenomenon: the out-of-town retail park, in which several massive stores are located in one area. The face of city centres has also changed, with shopping malls springing up within and outside towns, housing big-name chain stores.

The problem with supermarkets, malls and out-of-town retail parks

But what is so wrong with these developments? Surely having all the groceries you want under one roof is the most convenient and pleasant way to shop? I believe that there are a number of major problems with the modern experience of shopping.

Modern shopping is an unpleasant experience

Large supermarkets and shopping centres bring together huge numbers of people into one space. Although the buildings are often massive, there is still a feeling of claustrophobia. This unpleasant feeling is exacerbated by the way people behave. When we go to supermarkets, we want to buy our groceries and then get out as quickly as possible, as there is no reason to hang around other than to buy goods. So when we are in the supermarket we are in direct competition with each other, trying to get our shopping done as quickly as possible. This hardly makes for a relaxed and convivial environment.

A similar argument could be made for other forms of large-scale shopping – for example, because of the strong influence of consumerism on us (see Chapter 5), there is an air of self-absorbed obsession about people in shopping malls. They are immersed in the desire to consume things, and this desire is strongly self-focused. So once again there is likely to be little outward interest in, or concern for, others. These centres therefore seem to actively encourage us to retreat into our own shells and consider only our own lives and interests.

Large supermarkets and shopping centres can therefore be lonely places, with no real interaction between people – partly for the reasons mentioned above, but also because many are in out-of-town locations, so we are unlikely to bump into anyone we know there. Not only are they lonely places, but they also appear to encourage a fairly stressful psychological state of 'needing to get things done quickly' – another factor that contributes to our 'rushed lives', as discussed in Chapter 1.

The experience of shopping in a thriving local high street is quite different from the superstore experience, as one is not necessarily simply going with the aim to shop and get out as quickly as possible. Instead, it can represent an opportunity to walk around one's local community, get to know people in it, find out what is going on, and shop at leisure. High streets can also be places where we bump into people we know, chat and make plans with them.

Besides discouraging human interaction, the environments of large supermarkets and shopping centres feel artificial – from the bright lighting to the abundance of plastic. This type of environment makes the shopping experience even worse.

It makes us more reliant on the car

The out-of-town location of many shopping outlets now means that most people have to use their cars to get to them. Indeed, a government study in 1998 found that the distance travelled to shops increased by 60% between 1975 and 1990, and three-quarters of supermarket customers now travel there by car.[3]

Even if we ignore the environmental consequences of increased car use, we can see that it has a negative effect on our enjoyment of the shopping experience. It means that accessing the shops is more difficult for people without cars. These are often the poorest or most vulnerable, for example the elderly. Even for those of us with cars, shopping becomes less convenient as it may take some time to reach the location (especially on our ever-more-crowded roads) and then to find a parking space.

The process of driving can also be bad for our health, as we get less exercise and fresh air than we would if we had walked or cycled to the local shops.

It is not supposed to be convenient for us

A very important point that appears to have been missed by many people is that the idea of 'convenience', on which these large shopping developments have all been sold to us, is not all it seems. There is no reason why we should expect superstores and large retail outlets to be more pleasant or convenient for us than is necessary to persuade us to go back there again. These are not places planned or built for our convenience – they are there to maximise the profits of the companies that run them.

They are designed to get as many people as possible to buy as much as possible in as short a period of time as possible. It is about gaining greater efficiency in order to increase profits. Just as factories were developed in the Industrial Revolution to make production more efficient, which in turn maximised profits, these shopping centres have been developed to make consumption more efficient – they could be seen as 'spending factories' and we are the 'workers' whose spending they are trying to maximise! We even have to make the effort of travelling to them, in order to make it easier for them to get us to buy more! So, they are built for their convenience, not ours!

We are herded into centralised places with minimal facilities, in environments designed to make as many of us as possible spend as much as possible as quickly as possible.

It can threaten the environment

The development of superstores on out-of-town sites can extend urban sprawl and increase the threat to our natural spaces that was discussed in Chapter 2.

It threatens workers and farmers

Large corporations such as supermarkets and other chains operate within hyper-competitive globalised markets, which can create problems for suppliers as well as consumers. These include poor working conditions for factory workers, and prices for farmers and producers that may be even less than the cost of producing these goods.

The disintegration of the local High Street

The appearance of superstores, shopping malls and out-of-town retail outlets is not the only change in recent years. The face and character of our smaller towns has also changed.

In recent years we have lost a significant proportion of the small shops and services on our high streets. Research by the New Economics Foundation (NEF) suggests that within a decade the nation has lost nearly 30,000 independent food, beverage and tobacco retailers and that there has been a 28% reduction in the number of these stores.[4] Local branches of important services have been lost – banks have been turned into wine bars, and a large number of post offices have been shut down.

A big influence on this change has been the rise in large superstores. The same research found that large grocery outlets dominate the UK food retail sector, with an 81% share of the market in 2001. Tesco alone now controls a quarter of the food retail market.[5] Once a supermarket sets up near a town centre, it can suck custom away from independent traders in the town.

The buying power and dominance of these superstores enables them to pressurise their suppliers to lower their costs and to operate highly aggressive pricing tactics to undercut local independent retailers. For example, Corporate Watch note that in 2000, Wal-Mart was found guilty of breaking German law by selling a range of grocery items at below their cost price.[6] Many smaller traders just cannot compete with this.

There are many negative consequences of this change to our local towns, which we will now explore.

It reduces our range of local services

Some areas (for example, rural villages and suburbs) have lost almost all of their local retail outlets and services, which not only makes many services less accessible but can also suck the life out of communities. Reduced accessibility may simply be an inconvenience for some of us, but for people living in certain areas – for example, rural communities – it can have more serious consequences.

The decline in post offices is a good illustration of this. Between 1981 and 2001 the UK lost over 4,000 post offices – nearly 20% of all branches. A further 2,500 post offices are now under threat.[7] Post offices provide a range of important services for many members of the community – from post to financial transactions and advice. These services support local businesses and individuals alike. The closure of a post office not only causes great inconvenience for people – especially those who are less able to travel further afield for their services – but can also remove an important source of community cohesion. In a survey conducted in 2001, almost 90% of rural residents felt that post offices have an important community role.[8]

The loss of shops in a town may not be a gradual one – once the range and number of local traders drops below a certain level, it may rapidly force remaining customers to go further afield to do their shopping and speed up the collapse of the other local independent traders.

It reduces our choice of products

The dominance of a superstore at the expense of smaller local rivals not only leaves us with fewer options about where to shop, but it can also compromise our choice of products. Although superstores may argue that they can offer a wider range of goods, beyond the variations in packaging many products are standardised. They are also purchased from a limited range of producers – the organisation Grassroots Action on Food and Farming reported that the country's five largest supermarket chains deal with fewer than 30 major food processors, while the six largest retailers in the UK buy their milk from just four dairy companies.[9] On some items, a range of local suppliers may well offer greater variety.

It threatens the local economy, jobs and community

One might suppose that any jobs lost in local businesses as a result of supermarkets opening would be absorbed by new opportunities within the supermarkets themselves. This is not necessarily the case however: a study by the Competition Commission in 2000 examined the impact of 93 superstore openings. It found that they resulted in the net loss of over 25,000 jobs, an average of 276 per new superstore.[10]

And what about the new jobs created by the superstores? Many of these places are sterile working environments, and employees have the stress and insecurity of working for an employer that is solely focused on the ever-more-efficient pursuit of profit. Jobs may be less safe because superstores have no connection with the local community, and if they generate insufficient profits they can simply be closed down.

Local businesses are an effective way of keeping money circulating in the local economy. When our money is spent in superstores, however, we are putting it into the hands of national or global organisations accountable to their shareholders rather than to local communities. According to the New Economics Foundation, almost 90% of money spent in a supermarket will leave the local community.[11] The situation is similar in the United States: research from Maine shows that when $100 is spent in a large national chainstore, this generates only $14 of local spending by that store, whereas $100 spent in a local store generates $45 in local spending – over three times as much.[12]

The weakening of a local economy can not only cause businesses (such as shops) to close, but also change the very fabric of our communities.

Areas can become run down, with increasing crime rates. The loss of local shops can also contribute to a reduction in the cohesion of our communities, reducing our levels of social interaction and making us more isolated. We've already discussed the benefits of shopping in a thriving high street and the community bonds that this can form – including interaction with other people, getting to know the traders and finding out about what is going on locally. As we lose local shops, we can lose this social vibrancy and cohesion.

It reduces the diversity and identity of our high streets and towns

In many towns where high street shops have not been completely consigned to history, there has been the emergence of another trend – the arrival and domination of global branded chain stores, from cafés and fast-food outlets to clothes retailers. This has already turned many town high streets into homogenised, faceless arcades – 'clone towns'.

In some cases these stores have filled some of the gaps left by the demise of local retailers. In others, chains may have used their unmatchable purchasing power and influence to uproot local competition and establish a dominant position on the high street. This process may not be intentional in some cases (for example, when shop rental prices are pushed up in response to demand and local traders can't afford them), but its effect is always the same – to remove local competition.

In a somewhat ironic turn of events, the big supermarket chains themselves have capitalised on the decline in the high street (for which they were partly responsible) by building 'local' or 'express' versions of their own stores in place of local suppliers. 'Tesco Express' stores are already visited by over 7 million customers per week[13] and the company plans to build up to 1,200 of them.[14] These stores can pull trade away from local businesses in a similar way to their larger counterparts – one report from NEF suggests they can cause drops in business of 30%-40% for other local shops.[15]

Next time you walk down the high street of your local town, make a rough note of the proportion of truly local retailers versus the number of larger chains. You may feel that you live in a clone town yourself.[16]

As a result of this trend, the global is taking over the local. It diverts money away from local businesses to national or global firms and also reduces our choices. And it also threatens the character of our towns. Do we really want to see the distinct identities of our towns destroyed, so that they all become the same bland, sterile advertisements for global corporations? Or do we value diversity and character?

How has this happened?

A range of factors has influenced the growing spread of superstores and global chains, and the threats to local high streets. According to a report by NEF entitled *Ghost Town Britain*, these include:

> increasing market domination by – and preferential policy treatment of – super-markets; the failure to halt the 'downsizing' of banks and post offices; transport systems that encourage car travel; weak planning controls on out-of-town stores and a lack of support for truly local enterprise.[17]

A central driver behind these factors is the government's apparent inability to reconcile its faith in 'the market' with its attempts to promote thriving local communities. Government policy-makers have an overarching faith that economic growth (of any kind) will be beneficial to people and society, and that economic activity should be allowed to take place with minimal interference from the state. We will question this assumption more in Part Two, but for now we just need to note the government's willingness to allow supermarkets and other global brands to become 'invasive species' on the high street, without feeling it necessary to intervene to restrict their growth and stem the damage it is causing to people, local economies and communities.

This refusal to provide sufficiently strong regulation shows an inconsistency between government policies, as we now have a situation in which the government is investing large amounts of money in local regeneration whilst at the same time pursuing economic policies that destroy these very communities.

Chapter 4

'We're losing our communities'

Human beings have depended on their communities, local social networks and sense of place since civilisation began. In the modern Western world however, these local bonds have declined to the extent that many people do not know their neighbours or have much involvement with their local community at all. Not only is there concern about a loss of cohesion in our local communities, but also that the very essence of 'community' – the sense of belonging to a particular place and the feeling of being bound into local networks of people including family, neighbours and community groups – is being lost.

The decline of community

This section will consider our level of involvement with two important local groups of people – our families and our local communities generally.

Family

The typical family unit in the UK changed radically in the twentieth century, moving from the extended family living together or close to each other, through the nuclear family ('2.4 children and a dog'), to the growing modern trend for living on one's own. According to the Joseph Rowntree Foundation, in 2006 around 14% of the population in England lived alone – more than double the proportion (6.5%) that did so in 1971.[1]

As well as this change, ease of travel, improved communications and changes in work culture (amongst other things) have led many families to now become scattered, not just around one country, but across the world. Such families may only get together once a year, sometimes even less.

It is a sign of the times that many people view families as an annoyance rather than an important part of their lives. I am not suggesting that it is desirable to return to a bygone age of claustrophobic family ties with no mobility, but in an increasingly individualised and isolated society, we may be neglecting one of the most important sources of social interaction, support and love available to us.

Perhaps we should take a fresh look at what our families, and the people around them, can offer us. Apart from offering a ready-made social network, families can also offer the opportunity to get to know, and understand, people of a variety of ages that we might not otherwise interact with regularly.

Some societies have been able to retain their family-oriented philosophy longer than others, but even in some of these this fabric has begun to unravel in the face of economic and social pressures. In Spain, for example, strong economic growth and the burgeoning influence of a consumerist lifestyle have begun to change the face of many family set-ups. One consequence has been the flight of individuals from family homes to apartments on the edges of cities.

The local community

We now seem to spend less time in and around our local communities than we did before, and less time interacting with the people in them. As I have said, many people do not know their neighbours.

Many of us seem to spend our lives hopping in and out of our local communities – commuting to work, visiting friends in other places or travelling, rather than establishing a life or a sense of place in one particular location. Where we live doesn't seem to matter – we simply use the community as a base for our various excursions. And when we are at home, we might be too tired from these excursions to interact with others locally.

Of those people who do remain in their local community, many don't venture out but instead simply stay in their homes, engaged in inward-looking pursuits such as watching TV. Others feel the need to take refuge in their own homes for fear of local crime.

Of course, it could be argued that in recent times other forms of community have developed. The internet has led to the formation of vast numbers of 'virtual communities' in which millions of people from a range of cultures and backgrounds interact. It can also be argued that some of the social and cultural changes that have acted as influences in pulling us away from our local communities have been broadly positive – for example greater social mobility, more life choices and careers for women, and improved communications. However, strong local communities and a sense of connection to a place are important to us and our society in various ways, and we need to reverse this decline.

Research carried out by the Institute for Public Policy Research (IPPR) in three areas of Coventry in 2003 suggests that "a sense of local identity and attachment to place is something that many people value."[2] This does not necessarily mean we need to be best friends with everyone on our street, but it does suggest that "some people enjoy knowing that there is a common acknowledgement of their area being a 'decent place to live'."[3]

So what are the benefits of stronger local communities? The sense of somewhere being a 'decent place to live' seems to be less related to the physical environment than to the people, relationships and sense of community within it. One reason people feel better in such places, however, is that a sense of community can actually contribute to improving the physical environment. If we feel a sense of attachment to a place, we are more likely to care about the quality of the local environment, and encourage others to do the same.

Besides improving the physical environment, a sense of community can provide people with a number of forms of support and assistance. Rather than involving just co-operation between particular individuals ('reciprocity' – 'I'll do x for you if you do y for me'), an atmosphere of generalized reciprocity can develop – "I'll do this for you without expecting anything specific back from you, in the confident expectation that someone else will do something for me down the road."[4] This sense of community is not only pleasant to live in, but is also helpful for all who live within it.

Also, according to Robert Putnam in *Bowling Alone*, "civic engagement and social capital[5] entail mutual obligation and responsibility for action."[6] We are less likely to break our promises or unfairly take advantage of other people's co-operation if we are immersed in a network of strong social bonds.

This local engagement not only improves our attitude towards our local communities but also towards the wider world, as noted in *The Better World Handbook*:

"Our communities then become good models for caring about people around the world whom we may never meet – the beginnings of a global community." [7]

This is an important point: connection to, and involvement with, a particular place and people enables us to gain first-hand evidence of the consequences of our behaviour on other people and the world. It also makes us care about these consequences, because they directly affect us and the quality of our lives. It therefore forces us to take responsibility for at least some part of the world, and makes us more likely to extend this sense of responsibility to the wider world. If we don't have this local connection, we don't experience these effects or have anywhere that particularly matters to us and are therefore less likely to have this deeper sense of responsibility – either for our own part of the world or all of it.

Another important benefit of becoming involved with a local community is the trust it generates – not just of the 'I'll honour my commitments' type discussed above, but the reassurance that one lives in a place where one feels safe. Without this involvement, people (especially the elderly and vulnerable) can become even more isolated.

To illustrate this, statistics suggest that over the last decade or more there has been a decline in crime rates across the UK, most notably in street crime. Opinion polls however suggest that three-quarters of people think crime is rising. One report [8] suggests that this dichotomy cannot be explained simply by the media's obsession with violent crime, and that a further explanation could lie in the lifestyles of the two groups of people who felt strongest about the acceleration in street crime – namely the elderly and the affluent. The report argues that fear of crime has led the affluent to retreat into their homes behind gates, their cars and workplaces. In the case of the elderly, a reduction in opportunities for community contact (for example, the decline of local shops) has led to increased feelings of fear and isolation. Isolation promotes fear, which promotes further isolation.

The final – and most important – argument for involvement in the local community is that it is good for us. From the point of view of mental well-being, loneliness and isolation can be crippling. As Clive Hamilton notes in *Growth Fetish*, "The erosion of social connectedness . . . and the consequent deterioration of relationship skills lie at the heart of the [modern] epidemic of mental illness." [9]

According to the Women's Royal Voluntary Service (WRVS), 17% of people over 65 can be classified as 'socially isolated' – over 1.62 million people. [10] This statistic alone is sad enough, but it doesn't begin to convey the experience of the many people – throughout all age groups – affected by feelings of isolation and loneliness.

Getting involved in one's local community is a great way to reduce feelings of isolation and loneliness, and helps us to gain a sense of being part of a mutually supportive environment. In fact, as the *Better World Handbook* notes, a community should be even more than this:

> More than just a physical place, a community exists when people care for each other's well-being, share their lives, and embrace the ideal of loving others as they wish to be loved.[11]

In *Bowling Alone*, Robert Putnam (and others) claim that greater involvement with our community can also improve our physical health:

> The more integrated we are with our community, the less likely we are to experience colds, heart attacks, strokes, cancer, depression and premature death of all sorts.[12]

What's behind the decline in community involvement?

In this chapter I've suggested that the lack of involvement in our local communities has a range of negative effects, including increasing the isolation of some groups of people. The benefits of greater involvement in our communities seem to be substantial – so why aren't we getting involved in them?

The reasons are numerous and complex, but we can identify a number of likely influences. In *Bowling Alone*, Robert Putnam identifies several major factors that seemed to contribute to the decline in civic engagement and social capital in the USA in the last third of the twentieth century.[13] Although his focus is on the USA and on a more specific definition of social capital than the one we are using in this chapter, his points are a useful guide for trends in some other Western nations, including Britain:

Pressures on time and money

Our busy lives, our concerns about financial matters and the rise of two-career families have had some influence on the decline in community involvement, although probably only a minor one, as some of the negative effects are balanced out by the apparent trend for busy people to be more involved in the community than others.

Rising mobility and housing sprawl

The increase in suburban sprawl, commuting times and car use have also been contributing factors. Commuting in particular can reduce not only the involvement of individual commuters in their community, but also of other people in that community. Again, Putnam believes this to be only a small factor in the overall decline in community involvement in the US. We could add some further factors to this section for the UK, including the destructive influence of 'ghost towns' (discussed in Chapter 3) on community involvement, the shortage of buildings for community use and the gradual decline in public spaces such as urban parks.[14]

The development of electronic entertainment

Putnam's research suggests that a much more significant factor in people's retreat from community life in the USA over recent decades has been the rise of electronic entertainment, in particular television. The average American watches four hours of TV per day – one of the highest levels in the world.[15] Things are little different in the UK, however: in 2006 the average UK viewer watched 3.8 hours of television per day.[16] Not only does television pull people away from external interaction, but it can also isolate people from each other within their homes, as many homes have more than one television. Watching television can also induce a lethargic state in which one is less likely to get up and do something afterwards. Television steals time from other activities and lessens our willingness to get involved with the community or indeed, with anything. The development of other forms of (potentially solitary) electronic entertainment in recent years such as computer games and the internet must surely have exacerbated this tendency even further.

Generational change

Putnam argues that a much more important factor in the decline in community involvement in the USA than even television has been the change from a generation immersed in civic engagement to one that is simply less involved. He singles out the 'civic generation' born in the mid-to-late 1920s as a group who were particularly active in their communities, and that this involvement has decreased substantially with successive generations, including the 'baby boomers' and 'Generation X'.

The reasons for this are complex, but one key factor is that the 'civic generation' lived through the second world war. Patriotism and national unity against a common enemy were powerful binding forces both during and after the war, and this increased the civic involvement of these people as a result. It is reasonable to suggest that it had a similar effect in Britain. We have therefore seen "the replacement of a cohort of men and women whose values and civic habits were formed during a period of heightened civic obligation with others whose formative years were different".[17]

Besides not having gone through the experience of the second world war, are there any other factors that could have made subsequent generations particularly prone to disengagement from their communities?

The most obvious factor is the individualism generated by an increasingly materialistic and consumerist society. The consumerist age dawned after the second world war, and generations born into it have been brought up to believe that the pursuit of economic growth is the engine of the 'good society', and earning more and consuming more are key aspects of a successful life for an individual.

Such views are clearly inimical to involvement with one's community. First, they suggest that life should be focused on the pursuit of self-interest, even at the expense of others. This not only makes people inward-looking, but also suggests that life is a competition to outdo or get more than others, which in turn breeds distrust. Secondly, these views of 'the good society' and 'the good life' focus on goals such as wealth and consumption that have nothing to do with other people, relationships or community. It is therefore perhaps unsurprising that our social isolation has increased and community involvement has declined.

Chapter 5

'Consumerism dominates everything'

Consumerism is one of the strongest and most pervasive forces affecting our lives in the modern world. The term does not simply refer to immediate factors in our daily lives such as the omnipresence of advertising, but anything connected to the overarching idea in our modern society that in order to be happier, better and more successful people we have to have more 'stuff'.

In this chapter we will explore the power of consumerism, how it manifests itself in our lives, and the effects it has on us.

Advertising

Every day, each of us is bombarded with around 1,600 commercial messages.[1] This sounds like a massive number, but a typical day might feature the following activities: get up, read the paper (featuring advertisements), listen to the radio (advertisements), catch the bus to work (advertisements on the bus and at the roadside), arrive at work (advertisements on the internet), go home (maybe similar advertisements to those on the incoming journey), watch TV (advertisements) and go to bed.

Just take an example from one source: in a randomly selected weekday edition of *The Sun* newspaper[2] there are 41 advertisements, taking up roughly 22 pages of a 64-page paper. Over one-third of the paper consists of advertisements! This does not include the full page specifically devoted to classified ads, an entire section sponsored by a company, the prominent product logos in the sports section, or the other product placements that are included in many of the articles themselves.

We are exposed to advertising through a range of different sources. Some of them we may be aware of (like the examples listed above) but others may be less easy to spot, such as product placement in films. This is where advertisers pay film studios to feature their products in the films we watch. For example, a James Bond film might feature lead characters using mobile phones made by particular manufacturers who have paid a handsome sum for them to feature their product. For this fee, manufacturers would expect a few close-ups of the product's logo when the characters use it. One of the most famous cases of product placement was the use of the American chocolate sweet 'Reese's Pieces' in the film 'ET' in 1982. As a result of this placement, sales of the product increased by 65%.[3] Placement has now become so common that some films are being criticised for becoming little more than vehicles for a range of products. The 1997 James Bond film 'Tomorrow Never Dies' featured placement for the following products: Visa card, Avis car rentals, BMW cars and motorcycles, Smirnoff vodka, Heineken beer, Omega watches, Ericsson mobile phones and L'Oréal make-up. It's a wonder there was any time left for a plot.

However, despite occasional criticism, product placement remains widespread in films, TV programmes, magazines and other media. So commercial messages even affect how we are entertained.

But it goes further than this. In her seminal book on consumer culture *No Logo*, Naomi Klein identified a range of underground tools that marketeers use to get us to do things – tools that we cannot hope to identify unless we are insiders within the advertising industry. One example of such a tool is 'street promoters' – people who will "hype brands one-on-one on the street, in the clubs and on-line".[4] In other words, companies are attempting to recruit our friends and peers to sell us things – not simply influencing them to believe a product is desirable and telling us about it, but by actually paying people to use their status and relationships with others to flog their products to their peers. This is a rather cynical exploitation of human relationships and trust.

This massive amount of advertising is now such a normal part of Western society that most of us do not seem to realise just how pervasive it is in our lives. If you try to notice the number of adverts you see as you go through your day, and the sources from which they appear, you will discover just how much of your valuable time and brain space advertisers are forcing themselves into. Surely we have better things to do during this period of 'hijacked' time?

It is not simply the 'irritant factor' of advertising that is the problem however. Although we may have stopped noticing just how much we are being bombarded by advertising, it is still affecting our decisions, our world-views and our lives generally. We will consider just how much later in this chapter.

Consumerism – beyond advertising

But advertising is just the tip of the iceberg. There are many other influences in modern society that promote the 'values' of consumerism. To get a sense of these influences, imagine yourself as the recipient of 'mental inputs', the messages that enter your brain from the outside world. They could include the opinions of your friends, images from TV news programmes, advertisements on the internet and things you have learned from books or your education. Some of the major sources of inputs can be characterised as follows:

- Advertising
- Newspapers
- TV and radio
- Other media (e.g. internet)
- Workplace
- Family and peers
- Education
- Social activities (e.g. sport)

This is not an exhaustive list, but even if we only consider a selection of them we can see that many of them promote and support consumerism.

For example, newspapers and magazines do not just contain pages of advertisements but also stories about new gadgets, new clothes, property, makeovers, travel and many other things – all suggesting that having them will make life more fun and interesting, bring you greater freedom or bring some other positive change to your life. They may not promote an item directly in the way that an advertisement does, but many will help to create wants and needs in the reader – some relating to specific products like cars or clothes and others relating to particular ways of life that require further money and consumption.

Our modern obsession with celebrities also means that newspapers and magazines publish stories about glamorous people we might aspire to copy, and much of this aspiration is to indulge in the same things as they do – from designer clothes to private jets.

Overarching all of this is a tendency in the mass media (in the UK, at least) to be unable or unwilling to question consumerism as an idea. When this lack of critical thinking is accompanied by the promotion of consumerism that I have just been describing, this amounts to implicit support for it. Moreover, in their coverage of issues where consumerism could well be a major cause (e.g. poverty, climate change etc.) the media appear to be unwilling to make this link – somehow consumerism is regarded as an untouchable component of modern society. This applies to most mass media, whatever their political leanings and whether they are tabloid or 'quality'.

So it is not just the advertising within newspapers and magazines (or indeed other media – from radio to the internet) that promotes consumerism, but also much of their actual content. This content often includes features that directly create wants and needs in people; and also features that deal with topics that are apparently unrelated to consumerism but somehow still manage to give support to its vision of the world.

Leisure activity is another source of mental inputs. One example of a leisure activity that supports consumerism is sport – perhaps most notably football. Even at its most basic level – a kickabout in the park – the game is touched by consumerism. There is pressure on children (and indeed adults!) to have the latest boots, kit and the latest version of the strip of their favourite team. And clubs are well aware of the commercial value of people's loyalty to their team: many launch a new kit each year, with both 'home' and 'away' variants, along with numerous other items in their club shops. One of the most mystifying aspects of this is when fans buy an updated version of a team's strip that is no different from the previous one other than the fact that the sponsor displayed on the front has changed. This surely shows the power of consumerism – people being prepared to spend £45 to advertise your company for you!

At a higher level, football has become mired in consumerism and greed. Top players can earn in excess of £100,000 per week, creating role models for children that are not primarily based on excelling at the sport they love but on earning as much as possible and achieving a particular lifestyle. Football and consumerism seem to have become intertwined, and the same thing is now happening in many other sports, including rugby, cricket and tennis.

A final example of a source of mental input is our family and peers, who can influence us in subtle ways. Even sitting at home with one's family chatting about holiday plans, or in the pub with friends discussing someone's new mobile phone, can create new needs or feelings of pressure. Mixing with people who have consumerist lifestyles can therefore be a powerful influence on us. It can often seem as if this is the only way to behave, and that these are the only aspirations to have. In short, it is another thing that helps the consumerist philosophy to maintain its power in society.

The influence of other people on us can go way beyond friends and family however. If we look around and see that everyone is living consumerist lives with consumerist aspirations – from our neighbours to film stars to politicians – it is likely that most of us will accept this as the only way of life that is available, or if not the only one, then the best.

These are just a few examples of the many 'mental inputs' we receive, but in almost any area of life we can find consumerism wrapping its tentacles around us. Overall, this means that consumerism is the all-pervasive theme in our culture – a way of life and a judgement about what the best life is. It seeps into most parts of our lives, whether we are aware of it or not, and can profoundly affect us.

The effects of consumerism

It might be argued that we should have the mental strength to resist the influence of an advertisement or our friends, or that consumerism is nothing more than a minor irritant in our everyday lives. But this would be to greatly underestimate its power.

Exposure to even one advertisement can be powerful enough to influence us. Otherwise, why would Coca Cola alone spend $2 billion per year on advertising?[5] But when we are exposed to thousands of advertisements a day (and have been from childhood), and consumerism is promoted in most of the mental inputs we receive, we can become trapped inside a consumerist bubble which can mould our entire world-views, affecting our aspirations, views, lifestyles and many other things. And this trap is very difficult to escape from. Indeed, such is its power that we may not even realise we are caught in a trap. The real power of consumerism comes from its cumulative effect – the fact that it has seeped into every aspect of our lives, and that these elements of our culture continually reinforce each other.

Some of the effects of consumerism on us are what one might expect from a culture that promotes consumption. We slip into a cycle of wanting more things – whether it is the new iPod, another holiday abroad, or simply a particular type of food – and the pursuit of these things takes up our time, energy, stress and money (sometimes money we do not have – one reason for the spiralling debt of Britons today). We also constantly compare ourselves with other people (both real and fictitious), wanting to be like them or in their position. This leads us into a state of constant dissatisfaction – we are never happy with what we have, and are always on edge. And this is just what the logic of consumerism wants, as it makes us more active consumers on a continual basis.

Other effects are perhaps less immediately obvious but equally important. For example, consumerism can confuse us – especially when we start feeling that our lives are not providing us with what we need to be happy. We might have all the elements that constitute a good quality of life from a Western perspective – a job, car, house and other material possessions – but nevertheless feel somehow dissatisfied and empty, and that the pursuit of more possessions and the pressure of having to earn more money or sink into further debt to pay for this lifestyle is bringing more costs than benefits to our lives.

This situation can be extremely difficult to escape from, as there are very few voices in modern society that dissent from supporting the values of consumerism – even the mainstream idea of what it is to be 'ethical' still does not incorporate the idea of escaping the consumerist trap. Any individual struggling with a consumerist lifestyle is therefore unlikely to receive understanding, guidance or support from mainstream society – or from friends, if they too are immersed within this mainstream society.

There may well be millions of people who feel this sense of dissatisfaction in their lives but are not able to identify its cause or escape from it. Although consumerism is not the only reason why one might feel dissatisfied or stressed, evidence is building among psychologists that "holding a strongly materialist values orientation is, all else being equal, detrimental to psychological well-being".[6]

What's wrong with consumerism?

There is not necessarily anything morally wrong in buying and selling things, nor even in promoting them. But the extreme form of consumerism that now dominates the Western world has a number of unpleasant and even potentially dangerous characteristics.

It is intrusive

This is as good a reason as any to dislike it! Advertising, selling and product placement is simply an annoying imposition on one's peace and personal space. Advertising is everywhere, and spoils many experiences and pleasant views. It is like having a stranger following you and shouting at you for several hours a day.

It is manipulative

Both advertising and consumerism itself try to manipulate us into adopting a particular view of how we should live rather than letting us decide for ourselves.

One might argue that advertisements are simply there to make people aware of the products available to them and serve no other purpose, but this is not always the case. Many advertisements and other communications in our consumer society go way beyond this function, and attempt to manipulate people into making particular decisions.

Modern advertising is not just about telling people that a product exists – i.e. responding to an existing want or need someone may have. It is now about creating wants and needs that we might not have had before seeing the advertisement. In other words, it creates artifical desires and needs by manipulating us. The advertiser's ultimate purpose in creating these needs is always to make people want their product.

But how dare anyone manipulate us into having these wants and needs? If I really wanted to do something – say, purchase a particular product – I would decide for myself that I needed it and then make my own mind up about which product to buy once I had seen what products were available. If however someone tries to persuade me that I need a particular product and then attempts to create feelings of dissatisfaction in me if I do not have it, then this is an aggressive attempt to exercise power over me. This 'mental aggression' is just as unpleasant as physical aggression, because its effect can be equally, if not more, harmful.

At the end of his book *Authenticity*, David Boyle notes that he asked himself whether the book (about moving away from a society dominated by marketing, spin and fakes) was just for middle-aged people. He concluded: "Maybe it is, but I actually think a yearning for the real is shared by people far younger than me, because they don't like to be taken for a ride."[7]

It doesn't meet our needs

Some people may believe that living in a consumerist society makes them happy. But for an increasing number of people it does not. It creates impossible aspirations – quite simply, the principles it is based on make it a logical impossibility that it will make us happy. If the idea of consumerism is to continually create new needs in people and make them consume more, this will result in us constantly chasing after a carrot on a stick. Although we might reach it sometimes (e.g. by buying a particular product), a new 'carrot' (i.e. need) will then appear. A lack of fulfilment is therefore built into the whole idea of consumerism. This is not surprising, as the system is not aimed at meeting human needs and interests, but at generating profit.

The second point follows on from this: consumerism cannot provide many of the things that are important to us. This view is supported by recent studies in the relatively new discipline of 'human well-being' which is gaining increasing interest from politicians and others. It can broadly be described as the study of what makes human beings happy and fulfilled, and the desire to base political and social systems on promoting these things.

Research in this area is showing that consumerism is inconsistent with human well-being. The New Economics Foundation is a think-tank at the heart of this topic and in a discussion paper setting out the political territory of the topic they note that:

> The areas in which greater [financial] investment will yield continued improvements in well-being lie beyond the reach of markets.[8]

In other words, economic markets and consumption can fulfil some of our basic needs – including areas such as food and shelter – but there are other important things they simply cannot provide. The paper's author, Richard Reeves, describes these things as 'non-market goods'. As he notes:

> There is little wrong with Fabergé or Furbys. It is what [they are] failing to give us: companionship, time for reflection, spirituality, security, intellectual development and joy in our children.[9]

The problem is that consumerism often claims that it can provide us with these things. Firstly, advertisers link their products to real human needs. An example of this cited by Reeves is an advertising campaign for Doritos tortilla chips that linked the product to the idea of friends and companionship.[10] Secondly, advertisements will suggest (or at least, strongly imply) that the product can help to fulfil these real human needs. In the Doritos example, the advertisement seems to suggest that "buying their tortilla chips is one way to boost companionship, styling them 'friend-chips'".[11] Consumerism pretends to be able to meet our real needs – but it cannot do so. This process of misleading people about critically important human needs represents one of the saddest aspects of consumerism's manipulative power.

It has been encouraging recently to see the government and political parties beginning to develop policies to promote human well-being. Their efforts will never be successful, however, if they seek to achieve them within an economic system that continues to allow (in fact, encourage) the present culture of consumerism. The same could be said for attempts to address key global issues such as climate change and poverty, as we will see in Part Two. This is firstly because the culture of consumerism conflicts with the aims of human well-being (both globally and individually – e.g. poverty reduction and sustainable living) and also because it is so strong and all-encompassing that it makes it extremely difficult for people to see the inconsistencies within it or easily pursue alternatives.

It restricts our choices and lives

Even if consumerism did meet our needs, it would not be an acceptable philosophy on which to base our societies because we need to be able to make rational choices about the lives we want to lead, and it prevents us from doing this.

In its broadest sense, consumerism can be seen as a particular view of the 'good life' – a view that says life is better when you have more 'market goods' (products, services and activities). It developed as a result of a range of factors, including the desire for growth that is implicit within our global economic system, the need to get economies and societies back on track after the second world war, the technological developments of the last 60 years and the spread of new forms of communication.

But regardless of its origins, it does now represent a dominant view of how we should live. There are, however, many other ways we could live (e.g. simple living, or a focus on time and people rather than possessions), some of which people may feel are more appropriate for them.

There will always be one or more cultural systems that form the basis of society, and these will always feature a particular view of 'the good life'. I propose that we need a system that sees choice as a key aspect of the good life. Not the idea of 'consumer choice' that is so often presented to us in the modern world, but a system that enables people to have real choices about the lives they want to lead, gives them the skills they need to make these choices and encourages them to pursue the lives they really want.

Consumerism is completely inappropriate for this role, as it is a system that actually restricts our ability to see the choices available to us in life, make choices or put them into action. It only promotes its own view of 'the good life' – attempting to make people become better consumers – rather than helping people to see the full range of options open to them and helping them to decide for themselves what they want. It pretends that it offers people choices and freedom beyond its own view of the good life. You know the sort of thing: advertisements saying 'You're you. Be you. You can be what you want' and other such nonsense. But all that this is doing is encouraging you to feel free within the consumerist parameters they are setting for you. And that is not real freedom.

A key reason why it restricts people so effectively is that it has become a massively powerful force, with an influence across most areas of society and our individual lives. And as it is the basic culture of our society, very few people are going to be able to see beyond it.

It therefore becomes very difficult to question or escape from the consumerist world-view, even if one feels strongly that something is wrong with one's life within it. This is particularly difficult when consumerism claims to be able to meet all our needs, because it leads to self-doubt and confusion about our identity, happiness and life direction which is painful to experience and which, for many people, is never resolved. We will come back to this point about finding a culture that will give people real choices in more detail in Part Three.

It affects our world-views and characters

Consumerism has a significant influence on our perspectives on the world. For example, if we are spending much of our time and energy seeking the next product or activity to consume, we have less time and enthusiasm to learn about the world or broaden our horizons. Also, consumerism is unlikely to prompt us (or make it easy for us) to question important things such as the availability of the resources that maintain our lifestyles, the capacity of the planet to deal with the waste we generate, or the vulnerability of the centralised, import-reliant food supply systems that we currently use.

Also, consumerism plays a role in moulding our characters – perhaps in ways we would rather it did not. For example, if the whole aim of consumerism is to get us to acquire more, then it might well lead to excessive self-interest in the people affected by it. If it includes the pursuit of interests other than human (or value-driven) ones then it seems likely that those following this path will have less time for, or interest in, other people.

It is unsustainable

I won't go into much detail about this, as this book is focused on the current effects of the modern world on people's lives in the West. It is however amazing that the logic behind consumerism does not recognise the simple fact that the planet has a finite level of natural resources and a finite capacity for absorbing waste. It is self-evidently impossible for us to seek ever greater levels of consumption without there being disastrous consequences.

Final points

My aim has not been to suggest that everyone who tries to sell things to others is deliberately manipulating them for evil ends. Nor am I suggesting that consumerism was 'invented' by someone with malign intent – it is simply a cultural phenomenon that has emerged over time and that has a powerful influence in our societies and individual lives. We are all born into it and raised with it, so it is difficult to blame those who are delivering what the norms of the system say is desirable.

There are however many people who are escaping the hold of consumerism or are questioning the effect it has on our lives. And I would suggest that the modern form of consumerism has gone way too far – and is taking our lives, hopes and happiness with it.

Chapter 6

'We're not involved in politics'

Something seems to have happened to our involvement in politics in recent years. Turnout at the 1992 general election was around 77%. In 1997 this decreased to 71%.[1] But by the 2001 election it was only 59.4% – the lowest recorded level since 1945.[2] This rose a little in 2005, but only to 61.4%.[3]

This reduction in participation seems to have been accompanied by an increasing sense that politics and the political system in the UK are not offering ordinary people a real chance to influence political decisions. 90% of respondents to a 2004 survey by the Joseph Rowntree Reform Trust felt that 'ordinary voters' should have influence over government policies, but only 33% felt they actually did.[4]

This chapter will consider how and why our involvement in formal politics has declined. Some of the findings challenge a few commonly-held assumptions.

We've become disengaged

The statistics seem to say it all. We are simply not voting as much as we used to, both in national and local elections.[5] This is cause for concern, but does it mean we are any less interested in politics than we were? The research suggests not.

In the fourth *Audit of Political Engagement* published by The Electoral Commission in 2007,[6] it was found that just over half the public (54%) believe themselves to be either fairly or very interested in politics, a small increase on the first such audit in 2003 (50%). This still leaves a large number of people apparently uninterested in politics, but a different picture emerged when people were asked whether within the last year they had discussed any of a list of 17 local, national and international political issues presented to them, including Iraq, climate change and pensions. Only 6% said they had not discussed any of these issues in the last year.

These findings suggest that people are still interested in politics, although they might have quite a narrow definition of what the term means and, and in some cases, may see it as a separate thing from an interest in the issues themselves.

So apparently we are not becoming less interested in political issues; but is the fall in voting turnout evidence of an unwillingness to become involved? In another shift which parallels their changing interest from 'politics' to specific political issues, people may not be any less active in political issues than they were, but may simply have a different sense of what political involvement involves. A Home Office survey in 2005 found that 50% of British adults volunteer at least once a month, either formally or informally; this represents some 20 million people, and a rise of 3% from 2001.[7] People also engage in other ways: for example, according to The Power Inquiry in 2006, the percentage of the British population who had signed a petition rose from 23% in 1974 to 81% in 2000;[8] internet blogging has emerged; and the membership of many campaigning and advocacy groups, from Friends of the Earth to the National Trust, rose dramatically in the final decades of the twentieth century. The membership of the National Trust alone increased from 278,000 in 1971 to 3,000,000 in 2002.[9]

The Power Inquiry also concludes that "amongst the supposedly most apathetic – those who do not vote in general elections – 37% were members of, or active in, a charity, community group, public body or campaigning organisation".[10]

This evidence suggests that we are not necessarily less interested in politics, or less involved in it, than we were. We do however have a different attitude towards politics than we did, and get involved in a different way. The sharp decline in participation in the formal process of democracy, however, is still a serious problem. We need to be involved in these formal political processes because, despite the rise in other forms of involvement, they remain the only way to choose our representatives and to hold them to account. Democracy depends on participation, as democratically elected governments depend for their legitimacy on voters turning out to vote for them. Low turnout is likely to undermine public support for the political system and governmental effectiveness.[11]

Reasons for our disengagement

This section is based on the findings of The Power Inquiry, referred to earlier in this chapter.

Before we examine the reasons for our disengagement from formal politics, it is worth noting some factors that do not seem to be relevant. First, it has been suggested that people are voting less because they are 'contented' – i.e. their economic and political needs are being met. There appears to be little evidence to support this view, and if there were, we would expect people's involvement in all forms of political activity to drop, which is not the case.

Secondly, it has been argued that the dominance of the Labour Party over the last decade has led to a view that it is not worth voting as we know who is going to win, which has in turn led to low turnout at elections. However, people rarely give it as a reason for not voting.[12] Research by the Power Inquiry suggests that a more important factor is that under our current 'first-past-the-post' electoral system (where the candidate or party with the majority of votes wins outright), people feel that their votes in their local constituencies are wasted, because even in reasonably close general elections, the majority of constituencies remain safe for one party or another. If this is the case, we need to do something about the system itself rather than waiting for there to be more competition between the major parties in a general election.

Thirdly, it has been suggested that we now have less trust in politicians that we used to. In an era that seems to be peppered with political sleaze and spin this may initially appear to be a strong argument, but evidence suggests that the calibre of politicians has not diminished over the years. The Power Inquiry argues that "low levels of trust in politicians are part of a wider alienation from formal democratic politics resulting from more profound structural issues rather than its cause".[13] Some of these 'profound structural issues' will emerge as we now discuss some of the more convincing explanations for the drop in formal political engagement.

We don't feel that we're having an influence

There is a very strong feeling among the public that political decision-makers do not take our views or interests into account, and this belief seems to be an important cause of people's frustration with, and disengagement from, politics.

This belief appears to be reasonably well founded. In recent years there have been a range of initiatives that have purported to offer people the chance to 'have their say' on a wide range of issues, from the important to the trivial. But many of these appear to be somewhat feeble attempts to create the illusion that we have some influence. After all, 'having your say' on a poll, website or phone-in show is a pretty empty exercise unless it actually means 'having an influence' on policy. And this influence is rarely what is on offer.

Although these initiatives are springing up, policy-makers either ignore our voices on the things that really matter to us (for example, refusing to listen to the 1.5 million people who demonstrated in London against the invasion of Iraq on 15th February 2003) or restrict our opportunities to have a real say on important issues (for example, failing to have the promised public debate on whether to renew Britain's stock of nuclear weapons).

The concern that we do not have an influence on political decisions therefore seems to have some justification. We are offered poor substitutes for real influence – once again, the triumph of branding and style over substance – whilst being excluded from the real decision-making process. The assumption by those in power that we will fall for these substitutes shows such little respect for our intelligence that it only increases our feeling of alienation from political decision-making.

The main political parties are too similar

The perception that 'all the parties are the same, so why bother voting?' seems to be another factor contributing to the decline in people's involvement with formal politics.

A key factor in the blurring of the boundaries between the parties in the UK was the decision of Tony Blair and other architects of the New Labour project to place their faith in the financial market (and economic growth) as a means of delivering their policy programme, including social reform. This move disconnected the party from its socialist roots and brought it considerably closer to the other main parties – the only factor that really distinguishes them now is the degree of emphasis they give to different areas of taxation or expenditure.

This similarity in core economic policy made it easy for New Labour to adopt a policy of triangulation. This is the tactic of "shifting party policy into a broadly perceived 'centre ground' in order to increase electability and outmanoeuvre the opposition, who subsequently become associated with extremism and anachronism".[14] In other words, the aim is to make their basic values reasonably uncontroversial and to adopt policies that the majority of the electorate will find attractive, rather than policies driven by the party's own values and vision of a better world.

This strategy may have initially helped to make Labour more electable in the eyes of some people, but as they and other parties continue to pursue it, it may well have come at a price. To the public, it suggests that the parties are now more driven by the desire to hoover up votes than by a strong commitment to a particular set of values. This leads to a perception of the leading parties as shallow, lacking deep convictions or principles, and willing to alter policy just to get votes.

This lack of differentiation between parties and their lack of values has not only affected people's willingness to vote, but may also be one of the reasons for the decline in people's identification with a particular political party. A report by the Electoral Commission in 2005 noted: "In 1964 17 out of 20 people had at least a fairly strong identification with a political party. By 2001 only 11 out of 20 did so, and by 2005 the figure had fallen to less than 10 out of 20." [15]

Votes are wasted under the current electoral system

See the earlier point in this chapter about the weaknesses of the 'first-past-the-post' electoral system.

A vote for a political party commits the voter to too broad a range of policies

Voting for a political party requires us to register our commitment to a wide range of different policies, and we may not feel that any party represents our range of views with sufficient accuracy. For example, we may agree with a particular party's policies on health and education but not on climate change. This feeling that parties represent too wide a range of policies to represent our views accurately not only seems to be a factor in the decline in voting turnout but could also partially explain the relative strength of our interest and participation in single (or groups of related) political issues.

We lack knowledge and information about politics

Many people do not understand political processes and voting procedures (i.e. how to participate), and do not have a wider knowledge of what the candidates or parties stand for, or indeed of political issues themselves. This can put them off voting. For some people, this effect may be exacerbated by the decline in differentiation between political parties discussed earlier, as people have lost a shorthand way of making their voting choice (i.e. the Labour Party broadly stands for x, the Conservative Party for y), and the decision of whom to vote for has become more complex.

Voting procedures are inconvenient

Evidence suggests that this is a factor in the decline in voting, although it does not seem to be a major one. Some relatively simple changes could reverse any decline caused by this factor – for example, a survey of non-voters found that 44% said that they were 'very likely' or 'likely' to vote if they were able to vote by mobile phone or on the internet.[16]

The world has changed

It could be argued that none of the factors above is really new, as each has existed in some form before the current period of drop in turnout. For example, in the 1950s, the Labour and Conservative parties shared some very similar central policies, yet this period is viewed by some as a 'golden age' of formal participation, with high election turnouts and strong membership of political parties.

The Power Inquiry therefore suggests that there is a broader trend linking these factors. This is the fact that, since the second world war, Western countries have shifted from an industrial to post-industrial economy and society, which has changed us as individuals. For example, we are now less deferential to authority, old class structures and bonds have disappeared, and people are better educated and want to make their own decisions. There is now a substantial section of the population in Britain "that wants and requires a more regular, meaningful and detailed degree of influence over the policies and decisions that concern them and affect their lives".[17] And the current political structure in Britain denies them this influence.

Although this alienation is not necessarily confined to young people, its effect can be illustrated by the fact that the gap between levels of turnout of younger and older people has consistently widened since the 1970s. While in 1970, there was an 18 point difference between the 18-24 age group turnout rate (72%) and the 65-74 age group rate (90%), by 2005 the gap was 40 points.[18]

This shift to a post-industrial society has also exacerbated the social exclusion of the poorest members of society, leading to their increasing marginalisation from political life. As a 2006 report by IPPR notes, "Although there has been some decline in turnout among all income categories since 1964, the decline is most rapid for those in lower income groups. . . . Whereas in the 1960s there was around a seven-point difference in turnout between top quartile earners and bottom quartile earners, this figure had increased to around 13 points in 2005."[19]

It seems likely that the current period of disengagement from formal political processes came about when this collection of factors passed a tipping point at the turn of the 21st century.

The overarching problem seems to be that the British political system (and others around the world) has not adapted to these social and economic changes. The current political system offers a means of political decision-making and participation that is based on a social structure and a conception of an individual that no longer exist. Its system of elected representation and strong executive power was appropriate in an era where education was poor and people were deferential to authority, but this is no longer the case. The system was also built around the two major parties that represented the interests of the two main classes in the industrial age, yet society and the parties themselves have changed considerably since this time.

The overall effect of these factors has been to make people feel that there is little point in getting involved in politics; this is why people seem to have an interest in individual issues, but not in 'politics' itself. There is clearly a need to make some changes to reinvigorate interest and participation in formal politics.

Chapter 7

'The world is too large and too complex'

In recent decades we have seen some massive changes in the world: our knowledge of ourselves and our universe has increased, infrastructures have become globalised and technological developments have revolutionised the way we communicate with each other.

One consequence of these changes that has passed relatively unnoticed is that we have an increasingly complex world to deal with, which can affect us in a number of ways. Some of these may be detrimental to our well-being, and we may not have realised this.

This chapter will explore this increased complexity and consider the ways in which it has affected us as individuals. It will argue that we each need a new range of skills to deal with this complexity, and will discuss why we don't currently have them.

The complexity of the modern world

The range and content of information has increased

Human knowledge is increasing at an extraordinary rate: in 1965, Gordon Moore, co-founder of the technology company Intel, predicted that the number of transistors that could be fitted onto a computer chip would double every two years. Trends since his prediction have shown 'Moore's Law' to be reasonably accurate, and it illustrates the speed at which certain areas of knowledge are developing.[1] There is an increasingly detailed and rich resource of information about the world available to us.

Alongside this, the widespread use of computers and developments in communications such as the internet and satellite technology have opened up and centralised our access to a huge amount of information that we have never seen before. We can find out a great deal about what is happening in any country in the world, however remote, via the internet or digital television. We can look through the Hubble space telescope from our own home. Much of this information is updated almost instantaneously – we have a running commentary on what is happening on the planet (and beyond).

The range and number of sources of this information have also expanded beyond recognition – estimates suggest that the internet contains 15-30 billion web pages,[2] and hundreds of satellite television channels now exist.

This increase in information creates new issues for us. First, we run the obvious risk of information overload – there is so much information available that we are overwhelmed by it. This in itself can make us confused and anxious.

It can also be difficult to locate useful information, partly because sources such as the internet can give equal weight to any viewpoint or information provider, whether reliable or not, and the onus is on searchers to know exactly what they are seeking and the most reliable sources for it. The increased number of sources in other media (such as the range of television channels) can present a similar problem. We might not know the most reliable sources for what we are seeking, and in this situation might find ourselves using less credible sources. Useful information can also be hard to locate because one has to spend time negotiating layers of 'chatter' or 'filler' before one can reach it.

The increase in available information can also make it harder to identify which elements will be useful to us in our everyday lives. The wider availability of information with little differentiation of value between sources or types means that there is now less of an accepted 'range of knowledge' that is deemed to be useful for each of us to gain in life. People gravitate towards the 'niche' things that interest them, from celebrity culture to Cuban politics, regardless of whether these are as useful in their lives as other forms of knowledge (e.g. a broad knowledge of world history, or of how our food is produced). Whilst in some ways this is a positive thing, the decline of the concept of a 'canon' of useful knowledge to get us through life may be a problem – and a grounding of 'perspective' on some key issues would be useful for each of us, alongside the freedom and skills to explore the topics that interest us.

The range and content of communication has increased

Not only have the amount of information and range of sources increased, but so has the amount of communication being actively fired at us. In Chapter 5 we explored one such type of communication – commercial messages – but the full range we are exposed to is broader than this.

The range and content have increased for a number of reasons. Overall, we could simply argue that more communications are being sent to us through each source, and also that more sources of communication have opened up. For example, between 1995 and 2005 the overall volume of direct mail increased by 77%.[3] The reasons for such increases include the increasing availability and variety of technology to send and receive communications, together with the growth in commercial opportunities to exploit these channels. Some of this information is from interest groups, including environmental organisations, religious groups, political parties, government health departments and commercial organisations.

We are therefore subject to many more influences than we have been before, whether they are urging us to recycle more, give to charity, stop smoking or buy more chocolate. These often conflicting demands can cause us problems – how do we know which are the ones we should take up? How can we balance competing demands? Indeed, how do we know whether we should be following any of them at all? This increased range of demands can make us feel uncertain, guilty, stressed and envious. And we are given little guidance or support throughout our lives on how to handle such an array of messages and influences.

It is not just increased exposure to a wide variety of interest groups that can cause us problems, however, as the general increase in information we receive from the world can also present us with challenges. For example, the communication medium or information can be a nuisance in itself (for example, junk mail): it can reduce our peace of mind, and we might not know how to prevent certain communications from reaching us. We are also exposed to influences that are not necessarily from interest groups but nevertheless indirectly promote certain messages: for example TV channels will give us a particular view of the world, whether they are deliberately biased (e.g. reflecting the views of their owners), or simply reflecting the norms of society. Again, we are given little guidance on understanding these sources or how the information communicated by them could affect us, and this can result in our views being moulded (even if not deliberately), often without our realising it.

The complexity of the systems around us has increased

In recent years the supply chains, marketplaces and disposal chains for many of the goods and services we consume as individuals have 'gone global'. This has led to the development of a massive and intricate web of complexity behind even the simplest services we use or products we buy. For example, the ingredients of a typical BLT (bacon, lettuce and tomato) sandwich will have travelled over 31,000 miles and been through a huge array of complex processes before the final, simple product reaches the shelves of a supermarket.[4]

In the localised economies of old, the effects of an individual's actions were far less complex and extensive. The wheat needed to make the bread that they bought from the baker would probably have been grown in a nearby field, and any waste produced would have been disposed of locally. Although individuals have been 'plugged into' the global economy for hundreds of years, the difference in the last 50 years has been that our level of global interdependence has grown to a point at which it affects most areas of our lives.

Not only are there now more complex processes behind our everyday lives, but also a greater number of parties are affected by them. For example, when the ingredients of a BLT sandwich are gathered from a range of places around the world, a greater number of people (such as producers and packers) and range of environments are affected by this process.

This increased complexity in the systems around us presents each of us with new challenges. For example, it is difficult to tell who or what we are affecting with each action we take, and in what way we are affecting them. If we want to understand the effects of each of our actions (for example, if we want to live ethically) we need a great deal more information about the processes behind our lives than we ever did. And this information is often not easily available.

It is clearly too much to expect people to research, and then evaluate, this amount of information for every action they take. We may therefore be left uncertain about the consequences of even our simplest actions, which might make us feel guilty or anxious if we're trying to live in an ethical way. It may also heighten the sense that we are part of a system that is clearly wrong but is too large and complex for us to do anything about – a feeling that cannot be good for our well-being.

The complex processes behind our actions now also mean that even a simple action can cut across a range of different moral values that we may hold. A particular action may be consistent with some of our values but not others. For example, a t-shirt you are purchasing may be made from sustainable cotton, but the workers picking the cotton may have been subjected to unfair working conditions. In this situation, should the environment 'trump' human welfare? Questions such as how we should prioritise our ethical concerns are difficult, and if we don't know how to approach them, they can be confusing and make us anxious if we are trying to live in a reasonably ethical way. But, as we will see later in this chapter, no-one seems to be giving us guidance on how we should approach these questions.

There are more possibilities to choose from

As stated in Chapter 5, the 'choices' we are offered by the dominant culture of consumerism do not constitute real choice in the broader scheme of things. We should however acknowledge that there are a number of ways in which the choices available to us in our lives have increased over recent decades.

The increase in information available to us can broaden our horizons and expand the possibilities for our lives. This might be as simple as learning about new recipes from cooking programmes on TV, new hobbies presented in a niche magazine, new travel destinations gained from the internet or new political issues to become involved in.

For some, the possibilities might extend even further – falling costs of air travel and developments in communications have given many people the option of living in a different country, and in this respect the world has opened up to a proportion of the population. Developments in communications have made it possible for some jobs to be based away from the office in almost any location.

Overall, many of us seem to have more choice available as to how to spend the time in our lives than we ever did. But are we adequately equipped to deal with these choices? There are so many possibilities out there that it can be difficult to know which options we should pursue. Rather than being a positive factor in their lives, for some people the array of choices can be almost paralysing. It can also mean that we put pressure on ourselves, feeling that we should be doing more to make the most of the opportunities out there, even if what we actually want is to live relatively simple, quiet lives. The difficulty we face in making these choices is increased by the pressure that modern society exerts on us to live our lives in a particular way – to strive in life and make the most of every chance we have. This is explored in more detail in Chapter 8.

We need some help in making these choices. We need to develop the thinking skills and have access to the information that will help us consider which options are genuinely the best for us.

We lack the skills to deal with this complexity

The evidence so far in this chapter suggests that the world around us has changed to a point where we now all need a new range of thinking skills, simply to be able to live happy and ethical lives. We might not have needed these skills to such an extent in the past just to help us 'get by' in life.

Some of the skills that we need include the ability to gain perspective on our lives and the world around us, to think critically and to consider complex ethical questions. At present, the institutions around us such as our education system do not equip us with enough of these skills, or present information to us in the way we need in order to develop perspective on our lives and the world. In fact, as we will see, many aspects of the modern world are actually helping to prevent us from gaining these things.

Why we lack these thinking skills

We are immersed in detail, with little chance to see the 'big picture'

In the modern world, most of us live our lives immersed in detail, without having the thinking skills or information to enable us to reflect and 'lift ourselves out' of this complexity, in order to see our lives and the world in broader perspective.

As Chapter 1 pointed out, we lead busy lives in the modern world. We each have a large range of concerns and things to do in our everyday lives that can often lead us to 'keep our heads down' and 'just keep going', struggling to keep on the treadmill rather than getting off it regularly to stand back and see where we are going. We seem to lack time for reflection on any topic in our busy lives – even the topic of why we are so busy, and whether we need to be!

The influences and complexity of the modern world can also make it difficult for us to develop perspective and see the 'big picture'. On a daily basis we are immersed in so much detail, are surrounded by so many concepts and involved in so many complex systems (for example, those that produce and supply our food) that it is difficult to work out which sources of information will provide us with a useful perspective, rather than more unnecessary detail.

Another form of complexity that we are born into is human society itself, which has developed into a massive physical and conceptual structure over millennia of civilisation. The physical structure that human beings have built includes clothes, cities, buildings, roads and transport. Before the construction of this elaborate structure, we lived naked in the natural environment like any other creature. This *physical framework* is accompanied by a similar *conceptual structure* in which, over the years, human beings have built up a range of languages, beliefs, customs and concepts.

In both structures, some components are more important to us than others (for example, on the conceptual side, the law against killing people is more important than the rivalry between the Oxford and Cambridge boat-race teams). However, all of the content of both structures has been constructed by us over many millennia, starting from the simple position of us being naked apes. If we therefore want to see ourselves and our situation in some degree of perspective, we need to acknowledge that we are capable of developing these complex structures; but we should also be aware that they are human-made, and that major aspects of our identity as creatures are no different from how they were without these structures. Having this awareness makes us wiser people and less prone to arrogance and delusion in our day-to-day lives; but in the modern world, we seem to lack this important piece of perspective, and are not taught to develop it by the institutions around us, such as the education system.

The complexity of the modern world can not only make it difficult for us to develop this broad form of perspective about our status as creatures, but can also represent a barrier to developing perspective on a whole host of other, more day-to-day areas – from our impact on other people and the environment through to the sources of some of our cultural beliefs.

Nowadays the main institutions within which ordinary people reflect and think about broader matters are religious. But everybody should have the chance to learn about and undertake this process of reflection and thinking – not simply those people who belong to religious movements. Additionally, people should have the chance to do this thinking and reflection free from the influence of particular ideologies such as religions. The state therefore needs to play a role in providing these opportunities and skills.

We live in an 'anti-thinking' culture

Our lack of reflection in day-to-day life is not simply due to a lack of opportunities to undertake this process (although if we gave it a higher priority, it seems likely that we would be able to find time to do it). In the modern world there also appears to be a suspicion of intellectualism – an 'anti-thinking' culture, in which 'getting on with things' and 'taking action' are far more important and positive traits than thinking about things. The latter is seen as unnecessary and even lazy. This may be yet another trait that has emerged from industrialisation and the pursuit of economic growth over the last couple of centuries, as it reflects a feeling that people need to be productive members of the economic system, and that if you are not busily doing things then you are wasting time. It is difficult to step back and reflect or give time to thinking when most of the influences in our society are pushing us to keep our heads down, keep working and keep on the treadmill of modern life.

Life skills are not seen as useful knowledge

In a similar way to there being a preference for action over thinking, there also appears to be a preference for one particular type of knowledge over another.

Early on in his leadership, Tony Blair highlighted that the three priorities of his government would be "education, education, education".[5] But education for what? There is currently greater focus on educating people to become active, productive contributors to economic growth than helping them to develop other important life skills – including the thinking skills we have been discussing in this chapter.

In modern society, 'useful' knowledge seems to be that which will enable us to innovate, create, contribute to technological progress, develop businesses and make profits – in other words, knowledge that will help us flourish within the economic system. Whilst such areas of knowledge are not unimportant, they appear to be regarded more highly than other forms of knowledge, such as those in the humanities – philosophy, history, political theory etc. As argued earlier, however, this imbalance seems foolish, as the latter topics are key elements of the life skills and thinking skills we need to live happy and compassionate lives.

Education policy seems to be driven by good intentions but is heavily compromised by a conflict in priorities between economic needs and the need to develop healthy, happy human beings. It is clear that we need to rebalance our education priorities towards helping human beings to develop the skills (such as the thinking skills outlined in this chapter) that they need to live happy and fulfilled lives in the modern world, rather than simply addressing economic needs.

Knowledge is promoted above thinking

There is a tendency to feed people with detailed knowledge rather than to help them develop the skills they need to navigate their way around a topic and gain the knowledge they need themselves – in other words, the emphasis is on promoting knowledge rather than thinking skills.

This is something of a mystery, although it must be acknowledged that as our knowledge of the world and universe builds up, we need to focus on a limited range of topics in depth if we are to actually gain a thorough and up-to-date knowledge of them. This appears to be what has happened in academia, where post-graduate research in many topics now tends to involve working on a highly specialised subject in order to move forward knowledge about this area, often to a very small degree.

The ongoing advent of new knowledge does not seem to be a good enough reason to avoid adopting a generalist approach to knowledge in our everyday lives, however. To get through life, most of us do not need to have a level of knowledge of any topic equivalent to a PhD.

Perhaps the benefits of particular ways of thinking (including developing broad thinking skills) have not been recognised because of the reason highlighted a little earlier – because we have not allocated sufficient priority to helping people develop the skills they need to live happy and fulfilled lives in the modern world, which include abstract thinking skills. There may also be a view that some of these skills are too complex for many people to grasp, and therefore that they shouldn't be taught to everyone. This viewpoint lacks courage and vision, as people don't necessarily require an increase in the complexity of the content of the topics they are required to learn, but just a change in the skills we teach them in order to handle this content. Once they possess these skills, content that now seems complex may seem less so.

We don't see life skills as something to be developed throughout life

In the modern world, if people are lucky enough to have an education, they are only provided with a tiny sprinkling of all the knowledge available to them, and at a very early age. At the end of this schooling period, most people stop taking in this sort of knowledge in any serious way (if they ever did) and are then left to make their way in the world. Once we have left education, most of us go into jobs, and we try to do these – and indeed live the rest of our lives – with no reference back to the little we did learn at school, let alone attempting to gain more knowledge.

There is a strong argument in favour of increasing our focus on adult and lifetime education. It is already recognised by policy-makers that learning throughout life can bring us many benefits. But the identification of the need for thinking skills suggests that there are some 'skills for life' that we should be learning throughout life, rather than simply as children. Would a mandatory period of adult education in life skills be such a bad idea? Might it not only improve society generally but also reduce depression, improve relationships, increase well-being and have other possible benefits?

Summary

We're living in a world with different conditions from ever before – a world that has become more complex in various ways. We can often find ourselves 'lost' in this new world, with a high availability of information and various opportunities and problems tugging away at our sleeves, but without the necessary mental tools at our disposal to deal with them. This may be causing us a variety of problems, from ongoing anxiety and malaise to an inability to lead the lives we really want.

To respond to this changed world we need to consider what information each person needs to live 'well' (i.e. self-sufficiently and compassionately) and how to present and provide this information. We also need to give people a range of thinking skills which represent important 'skills for life' that could considerably increase their individual well-being as well as more effective thinkers generally.

Various aspects of modern society act against the development of these skills. It appears that policy-makers don't recognise their potential contribution to human well-being, and the overarching focus on promoting economic productivity brings biases and influences throughout different areas of society that make it difficult to gain or exercise such skills.

Chapter 8

'People aren't flourishing'

In the modern world, our identities are constantly under pressure. A whole range of external agents – including advertisers, family, friends, employers and governments – encourage us to think and behave in certain ways. It is difficult to defend ourselves against all these pressures, and once we open ourselves up to some of them, they can change us – often in ways we would prefer they did not. Many of the influences on us may be subtle, but they still affect the way we think and behave.

This chapter will explore how various aspects of our characters, identities and lives are repressed by the modern world. It will also consider how this has happened and why it matters.

Pressures on our identities and life goals

In the modern world, being yourself (and being happy with yourself as you are) is not enough. There are pressures from various sources (some of which are well-meaning) to develop ourselves, to fill in any 'gaps' we might have as individuals, or simply to become different people. There are also pressures to conform to particular identities.

At work

One example of this can be found in the work environment, where we are often encouraged to behave in particular ways, adopt particular attitudes and develop particular skills. Clearly, there are a number of specific skills that are essential in order to do certain jobs properly – for example, training in information technology if one is to become a computer programmer. There are however many other traits and attitudes that we are encouraged to develop that are not necessarily related to a particular job. These might include being highly organised, thinking ahead, not making mistakes, being efficient – generally being 'professional'.

This professionalism extends to the way we relate to other people. In our relationships with others at work we are encouraged to be pleasant but assertive – in other words, to form relationships with others but not ones so close that they might in some way put the business at risk. This view seems to regard human relationships as means to an economic end, rather than as ends in themselves. A good example of this is in the relationship between supplier and client – the relationship ultimately exists because each wants something from the other (the client wants a product or service, and the supplier wants a profit). Thus, however friendly it may be most of the time, if profits are at stake, the relationship itself is ultimately disposable and can be changed as required – it might become more aggressive if there is a contractual disagreement or if an invoice is unpaid. Long-term relationships are only nurtured in the hope that they will produce some benefit in the future. This 'work view' of a relationship is not what we would regard as a genuine human relationship. Of course, people do sometimes break through this and develop good, genuine relationships at work, but the economic imperative can all too often encourage us to behave in a different way.

This 'work view' of relationships also suggests that we need to be able to develop power over other people – to make them do things for us so we can achieve our goals. This may include buying our products, coming round to our views in meetings, or simply undertaking tasks on our behalf. This ability to gain power and manipulate is a central (although often unacknowledged) thread running through various forms of work training, such as 'assertiveness' and 'management skills'.

Most employers also want particular attitudes such as ambition and drive. These attitudes could be described as the willingness and desire to contribute increasing amounts of effort and commitment to those personal aims (such as gaining material wealth) that will in turn help the organisation to achieve its own goals.

So, at work we are encouraged to be the kinds of people who will enable the organisation we are working for to achieve its aims most effectively. In many cases this will be the aim of maximising profits, but it is equally applicable to organisations with social aims, some of which regard their staff as means to their social ends rather than actually being an important part of these ends. In either case we may be encouraged to become quite different from the individuals we actually are – for example, to treat relationships as if they are of little value in themselves but only as means to particular ends.

If we happen to possess characters or views other than these 'preferred' ones, then 'just being ourselves' is not enough for our employers – we are encouraged to 'develop' ourselves and fill in our 'gaps'. We might be given personal development training in order to help us develop various skills such as assertiveness.

This may lead us to wear a 'mask' to work. We put a great amount of effort into building up a persona that adjusts our characteristics to those required by our employers. This is not the real 'us'. To see an illustration of this in everyday life, consider what happens just after you arrive home from work at the end of the day – moving from your 'work self' to your 'home self'. In my experience, there can be a period of up to an hour where I am making a transition between the former and the latter – basically a period of 'taking the mask off'. Your partner or someone else you regularly see immediately after work may well notice a transition in you during this time of the day – if it takes you a few minutes to become the 'real you' again.

At home

It is not just at work that pressure is exerted on us to compromise our identities. There is a wide range of other areas in which this takes place.

The pressures on us to have a particular physical appearance – to be beautiful, thin and fashionable – have been well documented. There is also pressure to achieve a particular type of success in life – to reach as high a position in one's career as possible, to earn as much money as possible and achieve a particular level of consumption, and the status this apparently confers.

Branding also has a powerful influence on our identities. Companies want to secure our loyalty to their brands in order to maximise our custom and their profits. They go to great lengths to secure this loyalty, and the global success of some brands is proof of our addiction to them. The problem is that this addiction to brands threatens our individuality – we risk becoming mindless clones. We are 'mindless' if our behaviour can be dictated by whichever brand or company can spend enough to make it onto our TV screens or high streets. This is very passive behaviour on our part – waiting for the next popular brand to be fed to us – as opposed to the more self-determined approach of finding out what product genuinely appeals to us and seeking it out, even if it is a little harder to find than the most popular brand. And we are 'clones' because, if many of us behave like this, we will all be buying the same products, wearing the same clothes and aspiring to the same lifestyles.

Another example of a threat to our identities is the pressure to be a perfectly happy and well-adjusted person. Self-development or counselling can provide great help to people who are suffering, and give us the opportunity to develop aspects of ourselves. It can be argued, however, that we have developed too perfectionist a view of life. There is a belief that there is a condition of perfect happiness and 'well-adjustedness' that we should all be constantly striving for, and that if we are not 'working on ourselves' to achieve this, then we are somehow lazy and less worthy than others. This is similar to the idea that we should all be busy, productive and making the most effective use of our time, which was explored in Chapter 1. And if we are anything other than happy and well-adjusted in our mental lives, we are regarded as having a problem that needs to be ironed out. In extreme cases, a less-than-perfect mental state may be a terrible thing to experience, but for most of us life contains a mixture of highs and lows. Many of us have rough edges, feel confused at times, experience unexplained sadness, are better at some things and worse at others. This does not mean that we are failing or have characteristics that need to be ironed out; there is nothing to fail at, unless you have in mind a completely arbitrary view of what human beings should be like.

Yet another example of a pressure on our identities is the expectations that exist in modern society as to how we will live our lives. One such expectation is as follows: whilst all the complexity and influences of the modern have been building up around us, there has been an assumption that people will be able to adjust to them and deal with them adequately. Little attention has been paid to the effect these changes might have had on our ability to live happily, or to find the path we want in life. There seems to be an expectation that we will all thrive in this changed world, and that if we do not, there is something wrong with us. As we have seen, this expectation is misplaced.

Other expectations forming a backdrop to modern society include:

- That we will make the most of every choice and maximise every opportunity that we have in life

- That we want to see as much of the world as possible

- That we will know everything about the world, including other cultures, where our food comes from, political events, technological innovation and fashion

- That we will be perfect in every respect – ethical, lively, fun-loving, witty, reflective, gregarious, great cooks, nature-loving, intelligent, etc.

This list may seem a little far-fetched, but it is very easy to feel such expectations upon one's shoulders in a world where our exposure to the lives of other people has become so great. Through our increased level of global interconnectedness and improved communications, we can see the lives of other people at a reasonably intimate level, including politicians, professional sportspeople and individuals in other cultures. These represent millions of individuals who are completely different from us – they have different backgrounds and talents, have had different opportunities and made different choices in life. These could represent millions of possible lives to lead, experiences to have, expectations to meet and achievements to aspire towards. On reflection, it may seem obvious that we simply can't do all these things – but when immersed in our own lives, we can feel a pressure to try to embrace all these possibilities.

We are also sold expectations about our own lives – and not just by advertisers. These include the idea that we can be anything we want – we just need to strive for it. Whilst this can be a positive encouragement to realise one's potential, it can also have a negative side if we have not been taught how to establish our own identities, develop self-awareness and generally develop certain 'skills of living'. It can lead us to follow unrealistic paths, feel that we are owed success, or make us feel resentful or depressed if all our dreams are not fulfilled.

A fantastic range of opportunities and possibilities exists for many of us.[1] But the expectations that often accompany these opportunities can be harmful and make us feel that we are constantly missing out on something when we could just be living and enjoying the lives we have each chosen to lead. This in turn can make us flighty – hopping from one thing to the next, skimming the surface of each activity or experience and never being truly happy with, or immersed in, what we do. We need to develop the mental tools that will enable us to be happy with our own identities, to protect them and to be able to deal with the fact that we can't do everything.

The problems of a pressured life

The effects of these various forms of pressure to conform are manifold. If we feel that we are not accepted for being ourselves, this is clearly bad for our self-esteem and confidence. There appear to be standards of both how to feel and how to be as a human being that we are not living up to and that we must strive towards: these may be the status of our chosen career, material wealth, brand conformity, perfection as a happy and well-balanced human being, or any number of other things. This is of course utter nonsense, as it is entirely arbitrary to suggest there is a destination or 'ideal state' for humans to progress towards, and it is also impossible to define this destination for every individual – for example, what does 'happy and well adjusted' actually mean? We should at least start with being happy with being ourselves – warts and all.

Secondly, trying to maintain a mask, to be something that we aren't, is truly exhausting. Thirdly, it is highly stressful. At work, this stress may come from many things, including continually striving for ever greater 'improvements' in ourselves, attempting to keep the mask on, or simply knowing that we are expending this stress and effort on being a person we may not actually want to be. Outside work, it may result from the pressures of materialism and modern expectations of how we should live our lives – for example, feeling pressure to 'achieve' in work or to engage in every experience the world has to offer.

The 'perfectionist view' of human beings that we currently have adds to the misery. For example, if we are feeling unhappy at a particular time, we are likely to increase our anxiety and sadness by thinking that we shouldn't be unhappy, that we are somehow weak or wrong to be in this state and that other people are 'snapping out' of this state far quicker than us. We feel bad for being human. This perfectionist view also creates a culture of 'mental hypochondria' where we all feel our situation is worse than it is – when in fact we are just creatures trying to live life and make sense of things. One contributant to the 'modern malaise' we hear so much about might simply be the impossible, arbitrary standards we are setting for ourselves – among them the idea that we should not be experiencing any sort of malaise!

If we have been forced to wear some form of 'mask' in our lives (whether at work or beyond), a further danger is that, through regular use, it can become permanently attached to us. For example, we become the 'efficiency machines' we were trained to be at work, in every area of our lives, and thus risk becoming dull, uninspired drones.

These pressures can stifle many aspects of our identities, including our personalities, skills and happiness. If we are not allowed to pursue our own paths as individuals and feel happy with our identities, we are less likely to blossom and flourish – to do the things that genuinely give us pleasure and that make the most of the different qualities and skills that we each possess. We can also lose our sense of adventure, imagination, creativity and childish fun when we grow up within a society that is trying to make us conform to particular, restricted identities.

We are also in danger of becoming uninteresting. We become so locked into drone-like identities pursuing material wealth that we stop doing, reading, thinking or creating interesting things and therefore have fewer interesting things to say. We should be concerned about the type of characters that the pressures from work and materialism are pushing us to become – self-interested, greedy, manipulative, seeing other people as means rather than ends in themselves. Do we really want to become like this?

The exhaustion and stress that accompany our pursuit of these modern identities can also reduce our passion and energy in all areas of life. The attacks on our identities are slowly wearing us down, turning us into neutered, docile, uninspired masses.

The cumulative effect of this repression of our identities is clearly bad for our overall well-being – both mental and physical.

Summary

There appears to be a 'tyranny of identity' in the modern world. Various forces are stretching us towards different, sometimes conflicting, definitions of the kind of people we should be and how we should be feeling. These share the common sentiment that being ourselves is not enough. Most of them also happen to be arbitrary definitions of what a human being should be.

The dominance of these forces in our day-to-day lives means that many of us are not free to be ourselves, which in turn prevents us from flourishing as individuals. These forces can have many negative effects on us, from making us stressed through to turning us increasingly into uninteresting clones, for whom difference in identity is only acceptable within certain narrow parameters.

Why are we repressed?

Two of the most powerful forces influencing our identities at present are the drive for economic growth and the belief in human progress.

We have seen how industrialisation and the growth of capitalism have led us to form a particular view of time that has restricted our behaviour. These factors have had a similar effect on our identities. At work, the preferred identity is of someone who can make the most effective contribution to productivity, and thus maximise profits. Outside work, various other factors that constrain our identities have been driven by capitalism, including the dominance of branding and the emphasis on material and career success as the benchmark of human achievement. This is perhaps the greatest influence on our identities across the widest range of aspects of our lives.

Another influence has been the belief in human progress – the idea that human beings can 'improve' and that there is a standard that human beings should aspire towards. Although it could be argued that this belief has contributed to some beneficial developments in human society, it is based upon highly debateable assumptions about what human beings are and what it means to be human. The belief in human progress has been driven by both religious and secular forces, including Christianity (the idea that there is a vision of perfection for human beings to strive towards) and the Enlightenment (the idea that a human being and humanity as a whole can progress to perfection).

There will always be external forces acting upon us and perhaps seeking to influence us. Some of the forces in the modern world might be extreme and require regulation to ensure that they have less of a hold on us, but alongside this we must also equip people with the ability to challenge these influences and make up their own minds about who they want to be.

Part Two

The Causes

Chapter 9

What are the causes of our problems?

In Part One I painted a somewhat depressing picture of our lives in the modern world. Our material wealth is almost unimaginably greater than that of previous generations, but we also appear to face a number of pressures and problems.

Some of these problems may be obvious to us and some less so, but it is important to recognise the cumulative effect that these factors have on our world-views and our experience of life. A brief glance back through Part One suggests that many of us are stressed, pressurised, confused, lonely, isolated, lacking a say in the political decisions that affect us, and lacking the tools to stand back and reflect on our situation with a view to improving it. We seem to be a generation lost in the modern world.

We may have become so accustomed to this effect that we don't recognise it any more – we just feel its symptoms. These include tiredness, a sense of malaise and an underlying confusion. Having identified some of the problems, however, it is clear that they affect our lives in profound and dramatic ways, and that we owe it to ourselves to do something about them urgently.

Additionally, it pays to remind ourselves that the problems we discussed in Part One are simply those directly related to our own lives and interests as the supposed 'lucky ones' in the modern world – we have not even mentioned the urgent need to do something about the major problems facing the wider world in general, such as environmental damage, climate change, poverty (both domestic and overseas), human rights and many other issues.

We need to understand the causes of these problems.

The modern world

Perhaps the best way to understand the key causes is to outline how the modern world has developed in recent times.

The twentieth century was a period of world wars, superpower confrontation, technological development and social change. The second world war affected many aspects of global society, from the political (including the establishment of institutions such as the United Nations) to the social (including the attitudes of a generation towards community participation, as discussed in Chapter 4).

Following the second world war, large numbers of allied soldiers returned to their native countries needing housing, and to a society that reflected the contribution they had made in the war. This resulted in a period of major investment in social welfare in both Britain and the US in the late 1940s and 1950s.

The need to supply the demands of the war machine had provided a substantial boost to both technological development and industry, and the tools (and willing workforce) now existed to turn new ideas and the means of production towards satisfying the desires of consumers. A new era of consumerism was born. Fridges, cars, televisions and various other objects began appearing in greater numbers of households.

Technological change also gathered pace from the middle of the century, and has showed few signs of slowing since. This has resulted in some of the most substantial changes to our lives, including medical advances that have increased longevity (in Western nations, at least), changes in transport that have seen the massive growth of car ownership and air travel, developments in communications such as satellite technology, the internet and mobile phones, and changes in the way we are entertained, for example, the rise of television. The impact of these changes on our lives has not only been direct but also indirect: for example, as one of the factors in globalisation, it has contributed to an increase in the complexity of various processes such as those involved in supplying our food.

The last 100 years have also seen a major shift in social attitudes on a wide range of issues, including gender (women did not have a vote until 1918, and even then it was only given to those aged 30 or over), race, sexuality and disability. Linked to these changes is a changing set of expectations about life, what it holds for us, and how we are supposed to behave. In Britain, although various forms of discrimination still exist in practice, there is now a general sense that everyone should be given an equal opportunity to pursue the life they want, regardless of matters such as their gender, race, sexuality or disabilities. Such egalitarianism does not exist in all Western nations on all these matters. However, the importance of, and desire for, individual freedom, independence and self-determination has become a theme that has continually gained strength in most Western nations – and has been one of the forces leading to changes in certain areas of life, such as the increased fragmentation of households that was discussed in Chapter 4.

Our lives are also affected by changes in economic and political thinking, and the systems that underpin our society. Throughout the twentieth century, capitalism has been the dominant economic ideology driving countries such as Britain and the USA. For much of the century, the development of capitalism in the West was held in a form of ideological and global balance by communism, most notably in the Soviet Union and China. The break-up of the Soviet Union in the late 1980s was a sign for many in the West that the socialist experiment had failed and that capitalism had won the war of economic ideologies. The decision by China to open its system up to the market, and the country's subsequent massive economic growth, seem to suggest that capitalism is, as Jonathon Porritt puts it, "the only game in town" at present.

Capitalism is, however, a broad term, and it can take a number of forms. The particular brand that has developed and dominated over the last 25 years has been neoliberalism – "a loose grouping of ideas which indicate an emphasis on markets, very strong property rights, a smaller role for the state, balanced budgets and financial liberalisation".[1] It is a particularly strong form of capitalism that trusts the financial markets to deliver political, social and other goals and regards state intervention or regulation of any sort as unnecessary and harmful. Under this view, the central aim of a society is to make money, as this is the engine that drives benefits in all other areas. Neoliberalism actually goes further than this, suggesting that making money is not enough, but that constant economic growth is needed. We will return to the details of this system later.

This overarching drive for money and the belief in the benign power of economic growth has led to a number of policy developments in the global economy from the late twentieth century onwards, aiming to reduce government regulation and increase opportunities for profit-making – from the deregulation of national and international finance markets to the privatisation of public services such as the railways in the UK.

Another significant global change to have occurred in the late 20th century is that modern capitalism, in conjunction with improved communications and transport, has opened up markets across the world. This has resulted in goods or services that may have previously been produced in one's own country being imported from other countries due to the lower financial cost of doing so.[2] These goods and services might range from apples to the telephone call centres we consult for information about train times. This opening up of global markets and increased level of global interdependence is often what people mean by the term 'globalisation', and it has had various effects on our lives in the West. For example, it means that our 'radius of influence' as individuals has gone from local to global, and it is also a major contributor to the complexity of the world.

This form of neoliberal capitalism has set the overall context within which nations, and in turn individuals, operate. Interestingly, this agenda has been pursued not only by governments ruled by traditionally right-wing parties (such as those led by Margaret Thatcher and Ronald Reagan in the 1980s) but also by those with a progressive, left-wing background. It was the approach adopted by Bill Clinton's Democrats in the early 1990s and followed by Tony Blair as a central component of the Labour Party's transition to 'New Labour', through a policy broadly termed the 'Third Way'.

As Clive Hamilton notes in *Growth Fetish*: "Advocates of the Third Way looked for a means of grafting traditional social democratic concern for equality and social justice onto an economic system based on free markets."[3] Under this system, socially conscious governments have attempted to build stronger communities, improve education and health, and reduce inequality whilst at the same time placing money and economic growth at the top of their priorities and promoting the influence of the market. As we shall see, the conflict between the economic and social aims of this philosophy of 'neoliberalism with a friendly face' seems to prevent it from delivering its social aims adequately.

The three main parties in the British political system have all adopted a market-driven approach to policy-making, a move which has eroded the major ideological differences between them.

Alongside all these developments, another significant change has taken place: the Earth's population has increased from 2 billion in 1927, to 3 billion in 1960, to 4 billion in 1974, to 5 billion in 1987[4] to around 6.7 billion today. It is projected to reach over 9 billion by 2050.[5]

Common causes

Many of the factors mentioned above have played a part in producing some of the problems identified in Part One. But we can identify some key influences, and certain causes seem to be common to a number of problems.

1. Modern capitalism

A central cause of the problems outlined in Part One is the brand of neoliberal, consumerist capitalism that I have described. Indeed, this is such a central element of the modern world that when people refer to 'modern life' they often simply mean the modern capitalist system.

This form of capitalism is a rather extreme variety. It brings with it a single-minded drive for economic growth, a desire for as few constraints (whether for environmental or social reasons) on the market as possible, and the view that ever greater levels of consumption are the route to better lives.

Although it may initially appear to be a somewhat abstract and distant structure, the economic system within which we live has a massive effect on most areas of our lives, even those that we might imagine it doesn't touch. It influences many of the practical parameters of our lives, including our work, the property we are able to buy, our savings and what we eat. It also carries a number of implicit assumptions and values that filter down into a wide range of areas of our lives, rather like a tree diagram starting with one central strand that eventually splits off into hundreds of individual branches. It therefore also affects our world-views. The effects of consumerism on people and their world-views discussed in Chapter 5 is just one example of this 'filtering' effect in action.

The extent of its influence can be illustrated by a brief list of some of the problems outlined in Part One that it has had an effect on:

- *Chapter 1 – Rushing.* Current economic orthodoxy brings a particular view of how we should use our time – that time is a resource to be used as efficiently as possible and that we should therefore be busy. It also increases the intensity of our working lives as employers strive to get more productivity out of us

- *Chapter 2 – Natural spaces.* The desire for economic growth is one of the major pressures on government that can make it open to excessive influence from business interests such as the airline industry in the face of the need to protect important non-economic interests such as our environment

- *Chapter 3 – Shopping.* The pursuit of economic growth has influenced supermarket expansion and the growth of global chains that threaten the diversity and vibrancy of our high streets and the quality of local life

- *Chapter 4 – Communities.* It has contributed to the increased individualisation of society

- *Chapter 5 – Consumerism.* It is the central driver behind the whole culture of materialism and consumerism and its many negative consequences, including the removal of real choices from our lives

- *Chapter 7 – The world is too complex.* Economic globalisation has led to increasingly complex supply processes for the goods and services we use. It also contributes to a culture where certain types of knowledge are mistakenly valued and emphasised more than others and where thought and reflection are undervalued

- *Chapter 8 – People aren't flourishing.* It is a major force contributing to the repression of our identities.

It can be seen that our economic system affects many aspects of our lives, and it is therefore vital that the particular system we choose works for us. The current version is harming our lives. Although some of us are getting wealthier, we are not getting any happier as a result.

It is clearly desperately important to increase the income of people living in poverty, and as we will see later, the unequal distribution of wealth remains one of the scourges of modern society, even in the West. Evidence suggests however that once we reach a certain level of income, further wealth makes little difference to our well-being. According to a 2003 study by NEF: "Above a certain point – around $15,000 a head Gross Domestic Product – more growth stops delivering more happiness. An inside toilet makes you feel better about life; replacing a video player with a DVD player does not."[6] Richer people do not appear to be happier than those with a moderate income. Clive Hamilton found that "in the United States there is virtually no difference in reported satisfaction between people with incomes of $20,000 and $80,000. In Switzerland the highest income group reports a somewhat lower level of happiness than the income group just below it." [7]

To summarise the effects of modern capitalism on our lives: "The social basis of discontent in modern society is not so much lack of income; it is loneliness, boredom, depression, alienation, self-doubt and the ill health that goes with them. . . Most of the problems of modern society are not the result of inadequate incomes; they are the result of social structures, ideologies and cultural forms that prevent people from realising their potential and leading satisfying lives in their communities." [8]

So what is the source of these problems? Is it just the current version of capitalism, or is it capitalism itself?

There is little doubt that capitalism and its principles are firmly embedded in much of modern global society. This does not mean that it cannot change or be changed, but it does mean we need to investigate whether the solutions to these major and immediate problems can be found within the broad capitalist model, as wholesale rejection of the system itself is likely to be a long way off. We should also acknowledge that most of us are strongly committed to some of the principles linked to the capitalist model, including individual freedom and self-determination as opposed to a suffocating level of state control. So let us unpick some of the principles of capitalism, to see how far away we need to move from our current version of it.

The term is often used to mean slightly different things and can therefore be misleading, so let us break it down into some basic components, consider their contribution to our problems, and examine whether these are necessarily features of capitalism itself.

Markets

The term 'the market' has taken on a particular meaning in modern times: that of a weapon against state socialism and control, which should not be confused with the nature of 'markets' themselves. These existed for a long time before capitalism, but are a key component of it. They simply act as structures within which resources are allocated, often through the trading of goods and services. Whether it is a farmers' market in a village, a market in an African town or a financial market, it is performing the same function.

Markets are generally believed to be the most effective ways to allocate resources, and there is little reason to believe that properly regulated markets are problematic in themselves.

Markets can be structured and regulated in different ways, however, and some of the problems with neoliberal capitalism have been caused by poorly or unfairly regulated markets and by the deregulation of national and international finance markets over the last 30 years. According to Shah and McIvor, one result of this has been "a new economic climate of 'financialised capitalism' or 'casino capitalism' in which the requirements of contemporary capital markets, dominated by institutional investors, dictate that firms and governments prioritise short-term stakeholder value above all other considerations such as consumer needs, workforce development or longer-term corporate and industrial strategy".[9]

The most influential shareholders in large companies are often therefore not individual members of the public but investment firms. The only reason these firms are involved is to make profit – there is no other affiliation with the company, and they can exert considerable pressure on companies to increase profits at all costs (from job security at the company to its environmental impact).

The foreign exchange market is by far the largest in the world – its annual turnover has grown from $17.5 trillion in 1979 to over $300 trillion today.[10] Most money is based in speculation – essentially betting on how variables such as exchange rates will perform. Only 5% of this investment goes into new share issues,[11] in other words into the companies themselves. This not only creates a risk of economic volatility but also means that a key influence driving the health of the modern economy is not the people (or companies) that produce things but those organisations that gamble on what is going to happen to demand, exchange rates or other variables. This 'casino capitalism' has a major impact on us, as it means that critical aspects of our lives (from our pension funds to our jobs through to the price of food) are determined by the results of big-money gambling rather than the actual output of people or companies – gambling which of course has no regard for its consequences for people's lives.

We should also note that it is not necessarily useful or beneficial to open everything in human society to the market. The assumption that the privatisation of public services (such as health and education) makes them more effective is highly questionable. Market principles are not always the most appropriate model for running these services, partly because the services are about human beings rather than profitability, and also because the application of market principles can result in, among other things, increased bureaucracy and an overemphasis on targets that can stifle performance and drain morale – problems that many nurses, police officers and teachers will identify with.

Focus on financial capital

The sole aim of the current neoliberal capitalist system is to generate financial profit. The focus on this one aim in isolation means that all other interests are secondary to this and open to compromise as a result.

This situation is absurd. Human beings were the architects of this system, and we should be driving it, not vice versa. The whole point of having these systems is to make life better for us. But given the way in which the system currently functions, it has become an end in itself rather than what it should be – a means to our ends. And it is an end that actually conflicts with human and other important interests.

It seems peculiar that policy-makers would have devised the economic system to fit anything other than human interests. So why has it been devised this way? Although it may seem otherwise, it could be argued that the current system has been designed to meet human interests. The problem lies in the narrow definition of human interests that the system uses. Modern neoliberal capitalism (of the type followed by the major political parties in the UK since New Labour developed the Third Way) is based on a particular view of human beings and human nature. This is the view that we are rational agents seeking to maximise our share of goods, and therefore that freedom is 'the ability to get what we want'. This is an 'economic' model of human beings, where we are seen as calculating machines, and the market is seen as the best means of servicing our desires.

There are several major flaws in this picture of human beings. First, it assumes that we are fully rational agents able to make the right choices all the time. This is clearly incorrect – our choices and abilities to choose are influenced by external factors, including those caused by the dominant economic world-view. Nowhere is this illustrated more clearly than in the effects of consumerism in moulding and constraining our views and behaviour, as shown in Chapter 5. This view of the human also assumes that we have the right knowledge and information available to us to inform our decisions – again, something that is patently not the case. As we have seen in Chapter 7, the world is complex and we are often left to navigate our own way through the mountains of available information without a guide. We are also exposed to communications from various sources that seek to influence us using imperfect or biased messages rather than balanced factual information.

Apart from the inaccurate picture of our position as consumers, the neoliberal definition of human needs is a grossly inadequate representation of most of us. We are not simply self-interested calculating machines in the way the neoliberal model suggests – we are also social creatures who think of others, have sympathy, and actually need community and relationships. Not only does the neoliberal view fail to recognise these sides to our characters, but also the market (when financial profit is its sole aim) is unable to provide us with the needs that emerge from them – for example, relationships. We are therefore left with gaping holes in key areas of our lives, as illustrated in Part One.

It is clear that a flawed, incomplete view of human beings underlies the whole philosophy of neoliberal capitalism. We therefore need to build a revised approach to economics, based on a broader and more accurate view of humans, and pursuing an aim other than simply profit and economic growth – human well-being, for example.

It might be possible to deliver this within a broadly capitalist model. A central focus of capitalism is capital, which can be referred to as "a stock of anything (physical or virtual) from which anyone can extract a revenue or yield".[12] There is no reason why this stock should simply refer to money, as it can come in various forms, including social, human and intellectual, as well as financial. There is also no reason why the revenue or yield should be purely financial – for example, what if we evaluated it in terms of human happiness?

Profits and growth

The search for profit is a key aim of any capitalist economy. In the current model, it overrides any other consideration, including human welfare, the environment or anything else. As illustrated by the example of 'speculation' earlier, this appears to have led our society to become governed simply by the pursuit of numbers – the higher the profit, the better. This is clearly a major cause of problems in the modern world, as only the richest win at the expense of all others.

As to whether the pursuit of profit is a bad thing in itself, this is a topic on which political and social commentators are divided. To generate a profit, you need to have something that other people need or want, and be prepared to withhold it from them until someone pays you enough money for it to generate a profit. It could be argued that this principle is morally hollow as it acts against compassion – if someone needs something, should we not just give it to them rather than withholding it and exploiting them? On the other hand, there is a difference between people's (essential) 'needs' and their (non-essential) 'wants', and perhaps it is only the former that should not be exploited for profit. Perhaps we can find a system that addresses everyone's basic needs and then makes it possible to profit from their 'wants'.

It might be possible to have a form of profit that does not cause the problems outlined in this book. As we will see in Part Three, however, it will need to be strongly regulated in order both to ensure a fair distribution of wealth and to prevent the wealthy from restricting the lives of others. It will also need to take place within an economic system in which financial profit is not seen as the main goal, but is just a means to human, and other, ends.

A concept linked to profit is growth. In modern society the single-minded pursuit of profit might originally have been driven by the belief that economic growth was the panacea for all ills. Whilst this belief remains a central driver of our economic orthodoxy, the pursuit of profit seems to have detached itself and become an imperative in its own right – we now seek 'profit for profit's sake'.

Opinion is divided as to whether economic growth is a necessary element of a progressive society. The philosopher John Stuart Mill was one of the first people to advocate the idea of a 'stationary state' economy, which assumed that there were limits to growth and that, at a certain point, "the stream of human industry should spread itself out into an apparently stagnant sea".[13]

The desire to maximise anything in human society is normally based on a particular view of what is good for us. Such views often involve narrow and arbitrary views of human beings, and the systems resulting from them can encourage people to adopt particular forms of behaviour against their own choice, exposing them to familiar problems such as threats to their identity and putting them on a new treadmill. This 'push for progress' seems to be one of the more problematic aspects of capitalism.

Instead of abandoning any notion of growth whatsoever, one thing it could be in our interests to maximise in society is our capacity to pursue our own aims. This leads to a similar idea to the one noted earlier: that a more appropriate economic system would be one in which financial profit is not seen as the main goal, but as one of the means to an end such as enabling each individual to live a self-determined life. In this case, growth might not be a problem in itself, but the growth in question might not end up being purely financial.

Size

As far as the size of the economy is concerned, bigger is currently seen as better, which is no surprise given the modern devotion to growth and profit maximisation. Another area in which size needs to be considered is in regard to the scale of the institutions and systems: what size do they need to be in an economy to deliver its aims most effectively? Under the modern version of capitalism, the pursuit of ever-larger size is implicitly encouraged; the larger a company can become, the more power it tends to wield, as can be seen by the influence of supermarkets and global chains on our high streets.

This pursuit of greater size is an important factor behind some of the problems we discussed in Part One. For example, the growth of companies across international boundaries contributes to the complexity of the world. It is debatable whether larger companies are more profitable, but in any event, in an economy where financial growth was not the sole aim, other aims (such as quality of life and community cohesion) might bring a desire to scale down and localise some areas of the economy, such as certain elements of food production and supply.

Competition

This is a feature of any capitalist system, where 'competitiveness' is judged to be the difference between success and failure. If financial profit is the central aim of the system, this means that competitors will continually attempt to outdo each other to maximise this profit and go to any lengths to gain advantage. With no other criteria of equivalent value to profit, almost anything else can be sacrificed in the pursuit of competitiveness, including staff welfare, jobs, supplier welfare and the environment.

It is not only the fallout from this competitive behaviour that affects us. It also encourages the development of a competitive, individualist attitude in society generally – the idea of 'every man for himself', that 'it's a jungle out there' and that non-competitive, harmonious living is an idealistic, naïve dream. Attempts are sometimes made to justify these views by referring to the dubious ideas of social Darwinism, which suggests that the theory of evolution centres on a simple competitive struggle for survival and thus that it is the natural condition of humans to be involved in a state of aggressive competition with each other. This is a misunderstanding of the original theory, as it not only ascribes non-existent notions of competitive intent to genes, but also flies in the face of evidence of non-competitive behaviour in nature, such as interdependence, co-operation and the avoidance of competition through the development of niches.

As John Stuart Mill noted in the mid-nineteenth century, this artificial idea of extreme competition results in a pressurised, inharmonious and unpleasant form of society that is familiar to us in the present:

> I confess I am not charmed with the ideal of life held out by those who think that the normal state of human beings is that of struggling to get on; that the trampling, crushing, elbowing, and treading on each other's heels, which form the existing type of social life, are the most desirable lot of humankind, or anything but the disagreeable symptoms of one of the phases of industrial progress.[14]

There is little problem with competition in itself, as long as it operates within an economic system whose aims go beyond the single-minded pursuit of profit. If other aims such as the promotion of human happiness were placed at the head of the system, we would recognise the need to balance competition with other factors such as limiting the stress we each face (and which often comes from being in a constant state of competition) and promoting the pleasure we get out of close social relationships with others.

Private property

The principle of private ownership of property has the potential to be a problem if it leads to every square foot of land being privately owned. As I said in Chapter 2, we should not attach a price to many of our remaining natural spaces, as their importance transcends financial value. The private ownership of property may not prevent us from seeking a better world, but there would need to be tight limits set on it.

Deregulation

Under neoliberal capitalism, it is not only deemed important to 'leave things to the market', but also to 'leave the market itself alone'. Regulation is anathema to neoliberal thinking, as the unrestricted functioning of

the market is deemed to be synonymous with freedom. This idea of freedom often goes unchallenged and is often given as a reason to avoid reg-
ulating the market.

Freedom is a highly malleable concept. Freedom for one person to do
as they wish can often result in a loss of freedom for other people. Grant-
ing complete economic freedom to companies and individuals to make as
much money as they want can constrain the freedom of others, including
constraining our identities, our choices in life and our mental world-views.
As we will see a little later, it also constrains the lives of others all over the
world, and the environment.

As each person's claim for freedom brings competing claims from others, we must weigh up the two sets of claims carefully before we rush to
defend one or the other. We need to identify which of the freedoms under
discussion are most important, and prioritise the claims on that basis. At
present the freedoms of the free market restrict too many other important
freedoms and we need to rebalance this.[15]

We therefore need to reconsider our view of regulation. Rather than
being the attack on freedom that neoliberals would have us believe, the
regulation of economic markets needs to be 'rebranded' to signify something that promotes real freedom – specifically, a reasonable balance of the
freedoms that really matter to us.

Regulation does not have to be incompatible with capitalism, even in a
capitalist system based purely on the drive for profit. Although some
brands of capitalism (including our current one) would argue that a completely free market is essential, others may argue that a well-regulated
market is more successful.

In view of the above, the problem does not appear to be with capitalism *per se*, but with our current neoliberal version of it. This is a con-
tentious topic amongst people seeking social and global change. Some
people believe that the problems of the world can only be solved by the
fall of the capitalist system. I am however inclined to agree with those
(such as leading environmentalist Jonathon Porritt) who feel that there is
hope in a new form of economics that could still broadly be defined as a
form of capitalism, or at least maintains some of the main principles of
capitalism. It would look quite different from the one we currently have,
however, and we may feel that capitalism is not an appropriate term to
describe it. The new system could be driven by the desire to accumulate

forms of capital other than just financial (e.g. social capital in the form of more cohesive communities) and that is regulated with certain human and environmental concerns in mind. We will consider what this might broadly look like in Part Three.

A central concept within this alternative financial model will be sustainable development. The definition of sustainable development currently used by most policy-makers comes from the Brundtland Report, produced by the World Commission on Environment and Development in 1987. It describes sustainable development as "development that meets the needs of the present without compromising the ability of future generations to meet their own needs".[16]

Many commentators, however, argue that this definition is not wide enough as, among other things, it does not refer to the need to live within environmental limits or to seek a fair distribution of resources among people in the present. I firmly believe that a definition of sustainable development should encapsulate the overall vision of the better world we want to see, rather than one isolated area of interest, as each of us has a range of values we might want to see manifested in a better world, including environmental sustainability, less poverty, equality, social justice, quality of life and community cohesion. These values require compromise and co-ordination in order to reach the most suitable overall balance, so it makes sense to bring them together in a coherent overall vision. When I refer to sustainable development from now on, I therefore have in mind all these factors. The definition used by Forum for the Future, a leading UK sustainable development charity, will provide a reasonable guide:

> Sustainable development is a dynamic process which enables all people to realise their potential and to improve their quality of life in ways which simultaneously protect and enhance the Earth's life-support systems.[17]

Sustainable development policies are not sufficiently strong, broad or integrated at present, but it can be quite difficult to separate the effects of this from those of neoliberal capitalism, as under our current economic system sustainable development often acts as a counterbalance to the worst excesses of the market. A problem may therefore be caused either by the market being too strong, by sustainable development planning being too weak, or by a combination of the two. For example, from the problems discussed in Part One:

- *Chapter 2 – Natural spaces*. Although planning regulations for housing expansion have been reasonably firm to date, the same can't be said for some other land development projects, such as airport expansion. Whereas housing is essential, the decision to expand airports is a typical example of governments bowing to the demands of the markets ('if people want it, provide it for them') without adequate consideration of the broader consequences, such as the destruction of precious green space and increase in carbon emissions that more air travel will produce.

- *Chapter 3 – Shopping*. The expansion of supermarket developments and the development of many town centres into 'clone towns' domi nated by global brands have both been aided by the government's lack of willingness to intervene in the market, even when it is clear that it is damaging local economies and communities, and thus undermining other areas of its social policy.

In view of this link, the need for stronger, broader and more integrated sustainable development and the need for a new form of economics will be linked when we examine them in greater detail in Part Three.

2. A lack of the right mental tools

Another major cause of some of the problems in Part One is the fact that we are not generally equipped with the full range of 'mental tools' we need to live happy, independent and self-determined lives in the modern world. This is a vitally important point that has been missed not only by policy-makers but also by many people seeking social and global change. The world around us has changed dramatically over the last hundred (or even thirty) years, and along with it the mental demands made on us as individuals have both changed and increased.

As we have seen, the world has become considerably more complex and the pressure on our mental lives has increased. Of course, there were pressures on our mental lives in past times, such as religious indoctrination, but in the modern world these pressures are exerted in the context of an overarching belief that every individual should be truly free – and that these pressures on our mental lives endanger this freedom. Indeed, this belief is one of the forces driving me to write this book.

Not only have the mental pressures on our lives increased, but also the increasing complexity of the world has meant that we spend a greater proportion of our lives than ever before dealing with abstract things. For example, we are more reliant than ever before on information (and our ability to interpret and use it) rather than on the evidence we encounter in front of us in our daily lives. Another example is that there are more possibilities open to us in life, and with them, more expectations to deal with. (See Chapter 7 for more examples of the increasing role of abstract things in our lives.) We therefore need to become better at dealing with these things – whether they are in the form of information, increased options, greater expectations, or any of the other numerous abstract things that play such a big role in our experience of modern life. And to deal with these abstract things better, we need thinking skills.

What this means overall is that it has now become more important than ever for each of us to be better thinkers – not for any great elitist, intellectual purpose, but simply to enable us to navigate our way effectively through the modern world and to live the lives we want.

Despite these changes in the demands being placed on us, the mental tools we are given by parents, teachers and society do not appear to have developed sufficiently to keep up with them. There has been little consideration in our society of whether we need a different set of thinking skills to live happily and successfully in the modern world.[18] This can leave us without the range of mental tools we need, and this in turn can bring a range of profound problems to our lives, including leaving us open to manipulation from commercial influences and making us less able to cope with the expectations and demands placed on us.

This lack of mental tools affects several areas of our lives, including:

- *Chapter 1 – Rushing.* In general we do not have the critical thinking skills that would enable us to stand back from our lives and realise that the need to rush is part of an arbitrary view of what is important in life, and that we actually have a choice as to how we live.

- *Chapter 4 – Communities.* Similarly, we need the tools to be able to stand back from our lives and all the social norms and influences affecting us so we can decide for ourselves what is genuinely important to us.

- *Chapter 5 – Consumerism.* We need tools of critical thinking to be able to deal with the influences of consumerism and question the sources of inputs we receive in daily life. We also need perspective on the world and other mental tools to be intellectually independent and self-determined – to be aware of the real choices available to us.

- *Chapter 7 – The world is too complex.* We do not have the tools to deal with the increased range and quantity of information available to us, the increased amount of communication from the world, our increased involvement in the world or the increased range of possibilities open to us. We also do not have the thinking and life skills to get the most out of our lives.

- *Chapter 8 – People aren't flourishing.* We lack the tools to protect our identities, be happy with them and make the most of them amid the various challenges we face in the modern world.

The types of mental tool we need vary considerably. Some relate to specific areas of knowledge, some to critical thinking skills, and others to our ability to manage our thoughts so that our mental experience of life is a happy one.

In some cases, the mental tools are useful in their own right (e.g. in dealing with information), but in others they help us to unpeel layers of complexity to reveal things relating to our 'hearts' rather than our 'heads' (such as our values and what we want from life), enabling us to see them clearly. This process of revealing our true feelings is important, because the 'layers' obscuring them from us have often been built by influences from the outside world and our inability to manage them.

Of course, it could be argued that most of these skills would have been useful in any historical period. But we are now living in an age where the conditions, including social attitudes, affluence and democratic ideals, are more conducive than they have ever been to developing these skills.

I am not arguing that we should (or even could) try to turn people into purely rational creatures; instinct, intuition and feeling clearly also play important roles in the way we make decisions and live our lives. Nor am I arguing that 'mental tools' are a panacea for all our problems. I do however believe that these tools could help us to lead happier, more self-determined lives in the modern world.

3. Advances in technology and communications

As we have seen, technological developments have had a major influence on some of the problems outlined in Part One of this book. However, although it is a highly significant factor, technology is generally neutral in itself – it can lead to both positive and negative outcomes. The real determinant of its effect on our lives is the use to which it is put. The negative impact of technology on our lives can therefore be traced to other causes. For example, it is not necessarily the increased number of media that is the problem in consumerism, but the message that these media communicate. The cause of this problem is our modern brand of capitalism, not technology.

It can be argued, however, that technological development itself is a cause of the increased complexity of the modern world. The cheapness and availability of technology has opened up access to information and increased our mobility, both of which have made the world around us more complex and given us increased expectations. Yet they have also given us huge advantages. The solution to the problem of the complexity they bring to our lives lies in how we manage it, rather than extreme regulation of technological development – particularly as the latter is almost impossible to do in a democracy. What we need is to provide people with the right mental tools to manage the complexity of the world.

4. Other factors

Major events in the 20th century

Events such as the two world wars and the ending of the cold war had a substantial influence on the direction in which societies moved and the attitudes that politicians and public alike developed. There are however very few recommendations that we can make within the context of this book that will influence the occurrence and nature of such global events.

Social and attitudinal changes

There have been substantial changes in social attitudes over the last hundred years. It can be difficult to identify whether each of these is a cause or an effect – for example, the trend towards individualism. This might be seen partly as a cause in its own right (i.e. there has been a loosening of conventions and expectations around the individual, and a general increase in the feeling that people should be able to choose their own life paths), and partly as an effect (of factors such as consumerism, increasingly individualised entertainment such as television and the attitude of 'every man for himself' promoted by neoliberal capitalism).

The political system

The current set-up of our political system was identified as a major cause of the problem discussed in Chapter 6. Not only have we as individuals failed to keep up with the changes in the post-industrial world in terms of the mental tools we have to deal with it, but the British electoral system has also failed to keep up.

Religion and other ideologies

These play an important role in influencing a society's norms and thinking, but we do not have the space to discuss them in detail. Within the parameters under discussion, religion and ideology can be portrayed as another influence or source of messages that the individual will be better equipped to understand and make their own decisions on once they have developed particular mental skills.

Other modern problems

So far I have focused on the problems directly affecting the quality of our lives in the Western world. But the world as a whole also faces a number of urgent moral and practical problems, including climate change, the unsustainable use of natural resources and poverty.

The causes of many of the problems affecting our lives in the West are also the causes of some of our global problems. Before we consider this, let us summarise just two of these problems:

1. Poverty

Some 2.8 billion people live below the $2-a-day poverty line. There are countless sets of figures and depressing facts about global poverty that could be cited, but the following quote in a report by the New Economics Foundation sums the situation up:

That nearly half of the world's population should live in the 21st century in such poverty that up to one-third of their children die before they reach the age of five, at a time of unprecedented wealth among the world's rich, can only be described as a moral outrage.[19]

The issue of global poverty is of course not just about death but the suffering, deprivation and lack of power, voice or opportunities endured by those experiencing it.

Poverty also exists in the richer nations. For example, just under one in four people in the UK – nearly 13 million people – can be said to live in poverty.[20] This definition of poverty is used by Oxfam's UK Poverty Programme and is based on the 'poverty line' set by the European Union.[21]

The form of poverty in the UK and other Western countries may be different from that in some developing countries, but it can still strip people of their dignity, confidence, power and prospects in the same way. Serious inequality remains in the UK and some other Western countries, and its effects are more wide-ranging than one might initially think. As Clive Hamilton says,

It is well established that those at the bottom of unequal societies have less access to basic services such as good health care and education and that more unequal societies are more unhealthy societies, even if the average level of income is higher. In addition, inequality is responsible for greater social division, so that the rich and poor inhabit very different physical and social worlds and have little understanding of the other. It is also associated with differences in political power, so that the wealthy are in a better position to look after themselves at the expense of others. Finally, gross inequality tends to generate envy and resentment on the one hand and arrogance and feelings of superiority on the other, all of which lead to a less contented society.[22]

Inequality therefore exacerbates many of the problems we discussed in Part One – for example, the decline in voter turnout since 1964 has been most rapid among those with the lowest income.[23] It could therefore be argued that extreme inequality is ultimately bad for society generally.

2. Environmental issues

The environment is both a practical and a moral issue. We have only one planet, and this has a finite amount of carrying capacity – namely "11.5 billion hectares of biologically productive space such as grassland, cropland, forests, fisheries and wetlands."[24]

If everyone in the world were to consume the amount that we currently do in the UK we would need more than three Earths to produce the resources we would use, and to absorb the wastes we would generate. If everyone consumed at the US rate, we would need nearly five Earths.[25] To a certain extent the effects of our unsustainable behaviour in the West have been masked by the inequality in the world that leaves other countries existing on much less resource use. For example, if the footprint of Africa in 2003 was applied globally, we would need only 0.6 Earths.[26]

But despite the 'masking' effects of this imbalance, humanity has moved from using about half the planet's biocapacity in 1961 to over 1.25 times it in 2003.[27] We are already living way beyond the planet's limits.

The effects of our profligacy are there for all to see – we are running out of some of these natural resources. For example, it is predicted that we will reach the peak capacity of our oil extraction some time between now and 2020.[28] Fishing takes two and a half times more from the oceans than they can sustainably produce. And since 1980, an area of tropical forest greater than the size of India has been cleared for plantations, agriculture, pasture, mining and urban development.[29] The waste we generate from the use of these resources is also affecting us. Two major examples of this are pollution in cities and climate change.

Our global footprint looks set to increase over the coming years as the economies of other large countries such as China and India continue to expand rapidly – expansion that will be fuelled by ever greater levels of resource use, thus exacerbating the effects of humanity's unsustainable lifestyles even further.

The Intergovernmental Panel on Climate Change (IPCC), a body not normally prone to making exaggerated claims, provides a useful illustration of some of the consequences of our impact:

> The resilience of many ecosystems is likely to be exceeded this century by an unprecedented combination of climate change, associated disturbances (e.g. flooding, drought, wildfire, insects, ocean acidification), and other global change drivers (e.g. land use change, pollution, over-exploitation of resources).[30]

Environmental degradation also exacerbates the social injustice of poverty, as it is the poorest who are often worst affected by environmental change. For example, the effects of climate change are likely to affect the poorest countries most. As the IPCC notes, "New studies confirm that Africa is one of the most vulnerable continents to climate variability and change because of adaptive stresses and low adaptive capacity." [31]

In view of all this, it is clear that we simply cannot continue to abuse the environment in the way we have up to now – sustainability is a non-negotiable imperative for humankind.[32]

Causes

The causes of the global problems discussed here are clear. First, in a world in which there are enough basic resources to go round, poverty is a result of the unequal distribution of these resources. As the economic system is the mechanism for distributing resources in the modern world, we can conclude that its overarching philosophy and operation are a major cause of poverty.

At the heart of this is the continuing obsession of rich countries with maximising profits and securing growth. Although most rich countries are sympathetic to the plight of the poor, this sympathy (and their ability to do anything meaningful about it) is outweighed by the desire to secure growth for themselves and 'remain competitive' – both key doctrines of neoliberal capitalism.

As a result (so this thinking continues), developing countries cannot be given too much of a chance because they represent competition for the rich. They are also markets that can be exploited in the pursuit of further wealth. So, whilst some rich countries engage in well-intentioned efforts to assist poorer countries (for example, through aid), these measures are insufficient to relieve poverty as they do not redistribute enough wealth, and they take place within an economic system that is structurally biased towards rich countries. These countries seem unwilling to change, either to provide a 'level playing field' or to go further and give poorer countries some genuine advantages to help them address poverty. This effectively results in rich countries giving with one hand and taking with the other.

On their website, the World Development Movement (WDM) gives an example of a measure that promotes the interests of the rich rather than the poor:

> Rich countries are pressing developing countries to open their markets to competition, and to allow uncontrolled foreign investment. But no country in the world has developed economically without protecting and supporting its own industries. All rich countries still use these tools. Double standards, or what?[33]

Quite simply, rich countries are not currently prepared to take the economic 'hit' necessary to truly bring other countries out of severe poverty.

Resources need to be redistributed and trading rules need to be changed, even to give poor countries a level playing field, let alone to positively assist them in their development. The benefits of these steps will of course accrue to the poor at the expense of the rich – but this is the nature of redistribution and justice, and the whole point of rebalancing a system that is currently unfairly biased in favour of the rich. Although this would lead to a fairer world and everyone would benefit from it in the long term, the current brand of neoliberal capitalism seems structurally incapable of acts of significant compassion like this (or indeed of taking any radical step to promote any goal other than economic growth), as such acts demand the sacrifice of significant levels of their own economic competitiveness – something that companies and countries are loath to do under the current system, as it endangers their own position in an unforgiving marketplace.

The causes of many of our environmental issues are also quite clear: we either have too many people on the planet or we are consuming too much, or both. It is not difficult to identify that a key driver of our resource-heavy lifestyles is neoliberal capitalism and the assumptions behind it. For example:

- The belief that financial profit and economic growth should be the main aim in a society makes policy-makers unwilling to compromise it, even in the face of potentially catastrophic environmental consequences. The state's willingness to regulate on this issue is either too weak to achieve the necessary changes (as in the UK in relation to climate change) or virtually non-existent (as in the refusal of the US government to ratify the Kyoto climate change protocol because it would harm the American economy).

- Even when governments, businesses and individuals want to change their behaviour on these issues, they are often so locked into particular systems (e.g. the need for countries or companies to be maximally economically competitive) and the behaviour they encourage, that they are unable to take the necessary steps.

- The idea that increased material wealth is the path to the good life still dominates our society. Consequently, the idea that we should actually reduce our consumption remains absurd to the mainstream,[34] and the idea that we might actually be happier if we did this is regarded as laughable.

Neoliberalism is therefore incompatible with human or environmental welfare, as it is unable to compromise its main aim, the drive for profit and economic growth, for any other issue, however important it may be to the welfare or survival of people or planet.

Conclusion

The modern brand of neoliberal capitalism is therefore a major cause of global problems, including poverty and threats to our environment. It cannot be blamed for every global problem we face, but it is a central influence behind many seemingly unrelated problems, and its assumptions are not sufficiently challenged in modern society.

The basic principles of capitalism could be consistent with the search for a more sustainable and just world, but the economic system that would result would be considerably different from the neoliberal form we see today. There would need to be a new approach to economics: one that embraces the principles of sustainable development, including the needs to live within the capacity of one planet and to reduce poverty. A system where human well-being is seen in broader terms than the accumulation of material wealth, and where financial growth is not the principal aim. This is, of course, the same system as the one recommended earlier to address some of our problems as Westerners in the modern world.

The problems of quality of life in the West and the global issues we face are therefore two sides of the same coin. A more sustainable and fairer world would create the conditions for us in the West to live better lives as well.

As a final point, we should acknowledge that population growth plays a significant role in the issues of both poverty and environment. On a planet with finite resources, the more people you have to divide these resources between, the more strain it will put on these resources. This topic crosses a range of highly sensitive areas, including human freedom, reproductive rights and religion, and has therefore been a subject of considerable controversy since the days of Thomas Malthus, who in the early nineteenth century claimed that human beings ultimately had a choice between starvation or population restraint. Because of this controversy, many politicians (as well as individuals and organisations seeking social and global change) have been reluctant to mention, let alone tackle, the topic. It must however be considered as part of any vision to address poverty and environmental issues.

Part Three

The Solutions

Chapter 10

How can we change our society?

Having identified some of the problems we face, as well as their causes, we can now explore some ways in which we can make society in general and our own lives better – more compassionate, intelligent, exciting, vibrant, loving, authentic, happy and fulfilling.

In Part Two, I identified two major steps that need to be taken to improve our lives: implementing a new economics 'as if people and planet mattered' and developing an updated 'mental toolkit' for each of us. In this chapter we will consider what these measures might involve and the effects they could have on society.

1. A new economics

The term 'A new economics' might not suggest a particularly radical rethink of society generally, as it only seems to refer to our economic system. As we saw in Part Two however, the philosophy that underpins the choice of economic system also underpins the whole of society, including its priorities, its attitude towards the less well-off, its perception of human beings and human needs, and its view of what consititutes a good human life. We are therefore talking about a new set of priorities for society itself.

In setting out what a society with a new economics might look like, we will therefore start from some of these basic principles. Firstly, we should define the overall aim that our system of 'new economics' will focus on. We can use a description from an organisation that is driving some of the thinking on this issue – the New Economics Foundation:

> New economics is economics which puts the well-being of people and the planet first. Its purpose is to increase collective and individual well-being and to do so in a way that is both environmentally sustainable and socially just.[1]

There are many aims we could build our systems around, but seeking human well-being and happiness seems to be the most universally acceptable goal we are likely to find. Pursuing this goal within the parameters and resources of one planet is not negotiable – we need to regulate ourselves as a species unless we want nature to regulate us, and nature's regulation of us is likely to be somewhat harsher than our own! Finally, the need for social justice is not only based on the powerful moral view that extreme poverty and extreme imbalances of power are unacceptable, but also on the practical evidence that they are bad for well-being.

The next question to ask is what constitutes human happiness and well-being. To answer this, we need to have a conception of what a human being is and what is 'good' for us. As we have seen, this question can lead us into difficult territory for two main reasons. Firstly, we are nowhere near possessing a complete knowledge of human beings and what makes them happy; and secondly, different things seem to make different people happy. We cannot establish a detailed, definitive view of what is good for people.

However, as we have already seen, it is possible to identify some basic things that most people need to give them happiness and well-being. Health, for example, is vital to our well-being. Close relationships with other people are important, as are various forms of freedom, including the freedom and ability to be able to make our own choices about the lives we want and then to pursue them. And these 'promoters of well-being' require the provision not only of material goods such as food and shelter but also of non-material things such as community, relationships, mental skills and certain types of freedom.

I therefore believe that we should build our 'new economics' on a modest view of our knowledge of human beings and what is good for them – one that recognises that we are still learning about ourselves as creatures. There will, however, be some strong principles involved, based on historical evidence of the main factors that promote human flourishing, such as happiness, basic resources and freedom of thought and action; and those that prevent it, such as pain, poverty and slavery. It will also be a much richer and more extensive view of human beings than the one adopted by neoliberal capitalism.

This is a system that sees real choice as a key aspect of the good life. It enables people to have real choices about the lives they want to lead, gives them the skills they need to make those choices, and encourages them to pursue the lives they really want.

In summary, this new economics seeks to promote human happiness and well-being by equipping us with the basic material and non-material resources we need in order to live the lives we want. It will include a basic level of material goods such as food, drink, shelter and money, plus non-material goods such as the mental skills needed to be truly self-determined and live happily.

The new system will also promote particular conditions that are felt to be conducive to human flourishing,[2] such as stronger local communities, greater equality, education to promote well-being and the opportunity for children to grow without being exposed to influences (such as advertising) that they are not yet equipped to deal with. There will also be regulation to ensure that we live within the resources of the planet and within some boundaries of social justice.

The freedoms we regard as most important to preserve will be based on these foundations.

Interestingly enough, much of the basic structure of our society will be unaffected by a move towards new economics, as we are already getting some things right! For example, as NEF notes in *A Well-being Manifesto for a Flourishing Society*, "Government already does a great deal to promote well-being; the fact that we live in a democratic and stable state is an important prerequisite to our well-being."[3]

I do not think it would be helpful to place a label on the system that emerges from the new economics. Existing labels for economic philosophies (capitalism, socialism etc.) come with a lot of 'baggage', which can lead us into judging them before we consider them on their own merits.

Let us now explore some of the policies that might be adopted to deliver this vision of new economics, including those to secure the parameters of sustainability and social justice within which it would operate. The ideas discussed below should give a flavour of how the new system might work in practice.

Money, profit and growth would become means to our ends

The overall aim of the system is to promote human well-being, and therefore money would become one of several resources that will help us to achieve this aim. The economic system would become one of the suppliers of the material resources we need to live happily, and also help to fund other areas promoting well-being. This would not be its only role, however, as it could also provide people with some of the non-material goods needed to promote their well-being, such as social relationships and fulfilment from work. We will explore some of these benefits later.

There would also be an expansion of economic systems that don't use money as their unit of currency, such as Local Exchange Trading Systems (LETS), which provide a marketplace for people to offer skills, services and goods without money changing hands.

Under this new approach, the drive to acquire ever more money would lessen, and our ability to live happily and as we want would become the priority. This is a radical shift in thinking that could significantly change the way we view various other aspects of life. For example, we might become less jealous of other people's wealth when we realise it is not the most important thing in life.

In a new economy, growth would be a secondary consideration – the success of a society would be measured by its ability to deliver well-being within certain parameters of sustainability and social justice. Gross Domestic Product (GDP) would be replaced as an overall measure of success by a set of well-being indicators (see 'New measures of success' section later in the chapter). Whether economic growth is actually needed to sustain this kind of society is less clear. As we noted in Part Two, this is a topic that polarises opinion.

Following this change of emphasis, companies would have to play by different rules from those within which they currently operate. In a competitive marketplace (which would still exist to some extent) companies would compete to the maximum within the rules they were given, because if they did not they would be risking their survival. To change their behaviour, we must therefore impose changes to the rules by which they play. These changes would be imposed by governments and international institutions.

Although companies would still exist to make a profit, this aim would have to be accompanied by aims to promote well-being, sustainability and social justice. These would not be voluntary measures like those proposed by current corporate social responsibility (CSR) programmes, which companies are prone to interpret as a "ragbag menu of nice-to-do add-ons".[4] Instead they would be regulations that would change the meaning of what it is to be a business, and the responsibilities that come with it. For over a century, companies have enjoyed the same rights and entitlements as individual citizens without having the same responsibilities towards others. It is time this changed. From an ethical perspective it seems wrong to give them the same status as people, but if they are going to be given that status, at the very least they should be made to accept their responsibilities towards others and the planet, not just to their shareholders.

Specific standards could be set out for companies to meet in the promotion of well-being, sustainability and social justice. One standard of sustainability might be for every company to take responsibility for the whole life-cycle of their products – all the way through to recycling or disposing of them. A standard of well-being might be to ensure that staff well-being is monitored and meets certain requirements, such as job satisfaction and flexibility of working hours. Staff could not be exploited or unduly pressurised to achieve greater profits. If a company failed to meet these standards, it could be penalised by a regulatory body. In turn, corporate performance would not simply be judged on financial measures but also on these broader indicators.

Wealth would be redistributed

Under a system of new economics, financial profit-making would continue, but with greater levels of redistribution of wealth and with regulations to protect other areas deemed to be important, including the environment, social justice and other people's well-being.

This redistribution would take place at several levels: individual, corporate and global. We will explore the latter shortly, but for individuals and companies, a central component would be that people should have the freedom to live their lives and use their skills as they want. If they wanted to spend their lives seeking increased wealth, that would be acceptable. But the wealth of one person or organisation should not threaten other people's freedoms or the parameters of sustainability and social justice that our society needs to operate within. One way of achieving this would be to develop a significantly stronger taxation policy, raising taxes both generally and particularly for wealthy individuals and organisations.

This would have a number of positive effects. Firstly, it would help to reduce extreme inequality and enable capital to be diverted into improving everyone's well-being. Secondly, it would provide a balance to the additional power that often comes hand-in-hand with wealth, whether of individuals or companies.

Another aim would be to weaken the link between money and power. One of the most problematic aspects of money is not money itself – it is merely a medium of exchange – but the fact that its accumulation can generate power, which can be abused (e.g. by restricting other people's important freedoms).

However much we may wish it to be otherwise, some people will always want power over others. This would be the case whether the primary aim of society was making money or the promotion of well-being. We will have to accept that the pursuit of power is a constant feature of human society, regardless of the systems we use. We need to develop some mechanisms to stop its abuse.

It may be impossible to de-link money (or any valued resource) from power completely, but there are a number of aspects of new economics (including the removal of profit-making and economic growth as the main aims in society) that will help to reduce its influence. Action could be taken to limit profiteering on a range of items believed to be 'basic material resources' that are needed for a self-determined, happy life, in order to provide some control over prices and prevent people from experiencing shortages of basic goods due to speculation.

A significant redistribution of wealth would be undertaken on a global basis. In a world of sufficient resources, extreme poverty is caused by extreme inequality. We can give everyone enough to have choices in life. If we are serious about social justice, we should substantially redistribute money from the richest to the poorest countries – more than that needed just to address life-threatening poverty. We should be able to ensure that everyone has access to the basic material resources they need for life. This aim could be achieved by various means, including a recasting of tax systems – including the introduction of luxury taxes, taxes on speculation, inheritance taxes and ecological taxes, as well as a reinvigoration of progressive income taxation.[5]

I am not advocating equality of income. The new system should give everyone equal amounts of the same basic resources they need and then let them pursue the lives they wish, whether these involve striving to make large amounts of money or just 'getting by' and giving time to other priorities. To seek equality of income beyond this basic level would be to continue to make the mistake of assuming that money was the most important thing in everyone's life, and would also be a massive restriction of people's freedom – towards a 'command and control' economy. This idea of redistribution is clearly a major policy change, but we would be likely to be less worried about it in a system of 'new economics' as we would see that vast wealth is not the thing that brings quality of life for most of us.

Global redistribution would go hand-in-hand with a policy of fairer and more effective global financial systems and institutions (see below) in order to ensure that wealthier countries don't give with one hand and take with the other, wasting many of the long-term benefits of redistribution.

New measures of success would be introduced

If the pursuit of profit ceased to be the main aim of society, we would need to find new ways of measuring the things that matter, such as well-being and happiness. Currently, the UK government spends a great deal of money measuring economic and social indicators, but measures such as Gross Domestic Product (GDP) are poor ways of judging levels of well-being.

As NEF's *Well-Being Manifesto* notes:

> A set of national well-being accounts should be created which covers the main components of individual well-being – life satisfaction and personal development – as well as a range of components of well-being including engagement, meaningfulness, trust, and measures of ill-being, such as stress and depression. The indicators should also include measures of well-being beyond the personal, what we call social and ecological well-being – in other words, how we feel about and how engaged we are with the society and the environment in which we live. Well-being is not purely an individual phenomenon: it is rooted in our broader communities.[6]

These accounts would contribute to an indicator of a society's 'economic welfare', to replace GDP. An example of such an indicator is the Index of Sustainable Economic Welfare (ISEW). Jonathon Porritt notes:

> As well as adjusting for the loss of natural capital [a calculation that GDP does not include], the ISEW is also seeking to provide a better measure of welfare than GDP by adding to it some measures of un-traded benefits (such as unpaid domestic work), by subtracting the value of activities which are traded but do not contribute to human welfare (such as the treatment of pollution-related illnesses) and by correcting for income inequality.[7]

These 'new ways of measuring' would bring a range of benefits. They would help policy-makers to focus more on well-being and happiness, rather than economic growth as an end in itself. They would also help them to identify what policies could enhance well-being and help individuals to make better choices about their own lives.[8]

There would be a new attitude towards income and work

As I have said, everyone should be given the basic resources they need in order to identify and pursue the lives they want. The material resources could be delivered through the establishment of a citizen's income: a tax-free income paid to all people (including children) by the state regardless of employment status or social circumstances.[9] It would replace other forms of welfare such as child benefit, pensions and unemployment allowance. Such a step would have a number of advantages, including removing a large amount of the bureaucracy that currently surrounds the various forms of benefits, redistributing wealth and empowering people with a basic resource to help them pursue the lives they want. It would be paid for by the savings made from reduced bureaucracy in this area, plus new taxation (see earlier 'Redistribution' section), including taxes on speculation, ecological taxes and other progressive taxes to redistribute wealth, as discussed in the earlier 'Wealth would be redistributed' section.

It may be argued that this would create a generation of 'wasters and loafers', dependent on the toil of others to maintain their easy lives, and that it would lead to the collapse of society, with everyone choosing to 'loaf' rather than work. I make no apologies for the fact that some people might choose not to work under this new system, but that would be their choice, just as working to earn more material wealth would be the choice of others. And we should remember there are already people who choose to do less under the current welfare state system.

But in any case, the change in policy is unlikely to bring a major increase in unemployment. The citizen's income would not be a large amount of money. Unemployment is likely to continue to be extremely bad for an individual's well-being, and people will still want to work. The citizen's income might in fact encourage more people to work by reducing the level at which paid work would become worthwhile.

Resentment about maintaining any form of 'dependency culture' might well decline under the new system anyway, because profit will be replaced as the main aim of society with the promotion of well-being and enabling individuals to pursue their own life choices. Under these circumstances, those who were doing more paid work would have less reason to feel resentful towards those who were doing less, as they would each have made a choice about what they wanted from life and would each be pursuing it. If there were anything to become resentful about, it would not be money but other people's well-being, and as we would each be given control of our own lives, there would be little to legitimately complain about.

There would also be a new attitude towards work. We currently have a very narrow view of what useful work consists of – simply that which earns us individual wealth. This leads us to feel that work has to be a burden – something to 'put the hours into' before we can resume living our own lives during the rest of the day. Although the idea of the 'work/life balance' is sometimes useful, it is an unfortunate phrase as it reinforces the idea that work is something onerous to get out of the way each day before we can live life.

As we saw in Part One, however, work is an important factor in many people's well-being. It gives us a sense of purpose, another strand to our identities, new skills, more social relationships and a sense of achievement, among many other things. And work can be seen as much more than just paid employment – it can be regarded as any productive or creative activity that contributes to our well-being and that of society.

Most of us have to spend some time doing paid work in order to live, but under this new definition we can see that we also undertake many other forms of work, such as family duties, household work, creative activities and voluntary work. Many people would also regard some of these other forms of work as highly pleasurable and good for their well-being.

In a new economy, work and life would merge into one – we would not be led by the imperatives of economic growth and consumerism. We would therefore not feel obliged to spend as many hours as possible in paid work to pursue these aims, and instead would have a choice as to how to distribute our time between paid work, other work and leisure. We might decide to undertake enough paid work to give us the basic resources we need, and then balance this with other forms of work and leisure. Or we might decide to continue working longer hours in paid work; but this would be a choice, which it is not at present. Our range of choices in this area would be aided by our employers' commitment to our well-being, perhaps including a reduction, and greater flexibility, in our working hours. The citizen's income could also help us to balance these forms of paid and unpaid work.

Another change under a system of new economics would be the creation of better work – a policy linked to the need to set new operating parameters for businesses besides profit, such as well-being. Some of the principles involved in improving the quality of work are as follows: [10]

- As far as possible, jobs should be tailored to reflect people's individual strengths and interests

- People should be given autonomy – the chance to make decisions in their work

- Work should promote 'flow' (the state in which we are absorbed in what we are doing) – it should challenge us but not so much that it makes us stressed and anxious

- Opportunities should exist for interpersonal contact and the development of friendships.

Of course, some jobs would be very difficult to turn into stimulating, sociable and enjoyable experiences that lead to personal growth, but it would be possible to transform many people's jobs in this way. And surely it would be possible to improve even some of the most mundane jobs by promoting some of these basic principles.

A final consideration would be reducing working hours, but this would need to be accompanied by a change in attitude about work itself and its place in our lives.

A number of steps could be taken to reduce working hours in the UK, starting with signing up fully to the EU Working Time Directive, which attempts to set a maximum working week of 48 hours rather than allowing individuals to opt out of it. We could then move towards the 35-hour maximum week currently adopted by the French. We could of course go further than this, but the figures represent a maximum number of working hours, and at some point a balance would need to be struck between protecting people from exploitation and giving others the chance to fully engage in their job in a way that they enjoy. A 35-hour week plus greater flexibility to allow staff to work the hours they want might be the best compromise.

An additional benefit of reducing the number of hours of paid work would be that it would lead to a redistribution of hours towards people who are currently unemployed and underemployed.

Cumulatively, these measures could bring about substantial life changes for people. They might consume less as they prioritise other things above consumption and, rather than being controlled by neoliberal capitalism's idea of time, they would be more in control of their time and able to decide how to spend it. They would also have the chance to get off the treadmill of speed, and see work not as an intensive process of acquiring as much wealth as possible before retiring, but as a range of fulfilling and productive pursuits that are undertaken for their own sake throughout life.

There would be a new attitude towards time

People would be encouraged to consider their own relationship with time rather than being forced to see time as a resource that needs to be used efficiently. Indeed, they would be empowered to develop the skills to enable them to adopt this self-determined approach to everything – in short, to live authentically. These skills will be discussed later, in the 'Education' section.

Fairer and more effective global systems and institutions would be introduced

The new economics would seek to change the rules on which our global systems operate, for example:

- It would introduce economic reforms, including controls on capital flows. We saw in Part Two that, in global financial markets, a massive amount of money is spent on speculation on foreign exchange rates. Measures need to be taken to reduce the volume of these transactions, one of which would be to place a tax on them. This 'Tobin Tax' (named after a Nobel laureate for economics) has the potential not only to reduce the levels of capital flow but also to raise a substantial amount of money to put towards policies to promote social justice (such as cancelling the unpayable debts of poor countries) and sustainability.

- It would establish fair trading conditions for developing countries in the global marketplace. Following on from Part Two, there is a strong argument for actually giving advantages to developing countries until they have put their economies onto a stable footing and are able to join the global market without such support. One such advantage would be to allow them to develop some or all elements of their markets behind trade barriers to protect them whilst enjoying open access to the markets of developed countries. In addition, developed countries should allow developing countries to do this without any strings attached, and without forcing them to follow the specific model of economic development preferred by developed countries.

This idea of fairer global trading conditions could be seen as the global component of a policy to promote the strength of local economies, whether of local towns or of developing countries. We will examine how economic localisation might look at a national level later. For now, I would just like to reinforce the point that this policy aims to ensure that the power of the wealthy does not enable them to threaten the most important freedoms of others. And at each level, a combination of stronger taxation and selected regulation may be the way to deliver this aim.

There is debate within the environmental movement as to whether a better world could be achieved through a process of localisation (i.e. making local economies as self-sufficient as possible and relying on sources close to home for their survival) or through reform of the global system to make it more sustainable. I believe that both need to happen. First, we need to promote local economies, partly to enable individual towns and nations to thrive and retain their identities and cultures, and also to reduce the level of environmental impact of some global processes, such as the 31,000-mile journey of the typical supermarket BLT sandwich. Global interconnection and trade would still be features of our world, but there would be a rebalancing to promote the local too. Secondly, we need to reform the global system and the institutions within it in order to make them compatible with a new economics and to ensure that they have the scope and strength to enforce regulation when they need to – whether applied to global corporations or to governments.

We therefore need to improve international institutions. A wide range of ideas and proposals has been put forward by various individuals and organisations on how to do this, but essentially, under new economics, institutions such as the World Trade Organisation (WTO) would be reformed to promote and enforce the philosophy and policies of new economics rather than those of neoliberal capitalism that they currently support.

New institutions might also need to be created (or existing ones such as the UN extended and strengthened) to govern issues such as global sustainability.

Sustainability would be a central aim

There is a wide range of principles and policies that could deliver this aim. At a global level, one measure that could be undertaken to encourage the development of environmentally sustainable products, services and practices is the introduction of environmental taxes so that prices of goods and services reflected their full environmental cost. These should not act as taxes on the poor however – there should be enough money raised from the taxes to provide rebates to the less well-off. We are already beginning to see that there is a whole host of opportunities to profitably develop new products, services and industries that are based on sustainability, from the development of sustainable technology to organic food through to ecological home design.

Another global measure would be to set high environmental standards for companies, making them responsible for the materials and output they produce, both in their products and services and in their production. Policies might include zero-emission production, making companies take responsibility for the materials they use over their whole lifetime, and making products that are fully recyclable. This sustainable approach to business should be promoted in all areas of life, leading us towards a society where sustainability is second nature rather than a chore.

There would also be international agreements on our use of environmental resources. One of the most promising ideas in this area is called 'Contraction and Convergence', in which a 'carbon budget' is set for all nations, based on a per capita allocation of allowable emissions. Under this system, nations with more carbon usage (usually the rich ones) would be able to buy carbon credits from poorer nations which had operated within their 'carbon budget'. As time progressed, the development of the poorer countries might lead to an increase in their levels of carbon emissions, which would leave them with fewer carbon credits to sell to the richer countries. These would then have to cut back their emissions further, eventually leading to a convergence in the per capita levels of these countries. This scheme neatly brings together the ideas of sustainability and social justice, as everyone in the world is allocated the same individual carbon budget, and this could shift a reasonable level of resources from rich to poor countries.

In the system I am suggesting, it would not only be our carbon use that would be rationed, but our use of natural resources generally, in order to encourage one-planet living. Carbon emissions, although extremely important, represent just one area of the environment in which we are living beyond our means. We should each be issued with an allocation of global resources (i.e. a particular 'global footprint') that we must live within, and follow the same procedure of trading as in the contraction and convergence programme.

On a national level, the government's sustainable development strategy would avoid many of the existing contradictions in its policies, such as promoting airport expansion whilst attempting to substantially reduce carbon emissions.

The government needs to exercise more 'joined-up thinking' on sustainable development, in order to ensure that policies are consistent across all areas of life. For example, it would be difficult to reduce car use significantly unless an integrated set of policies were adopted across a range of areas of government policy, including the provision of better public transport, stronger local economies and high streets, road pricing, and the building of new towns designed for car-free rather than car-reliant living.

A sustainable development policy under a system of new economics would provide firm protection for threatened natural spaces by adopting a precautionary approach and assigning protected status to more land. It would aim to reduce the threat itself, although the demand for new land for development would continue even under such a system. Policies that would help to reduce the threat to our natural spaces include making better use of 'brownfield' land, making use of the nearly 700,000 empty homes in England alone, encouraging urban regeneration, limiting home ownership to one per person, reducing car use and aviation through environmental taxation, and a halt to airport expansion.

We also need to consider the issue of population growth. One of the advantages of allocating every individual a level of permitted 'global footprint' is that people would become more aware of the forces affecting their allocation, from those driving it up (such as increasing technological efficiency) to those driving it down (such as growing global population levels). An awareness that growing population levels are reducing everyone's share of the planet may be one of the starkest and most effective ways of encouraging policies to address the issue of population growth.

Many of the suggestions put forward in this chapter to address other areas such as global social justice also have the potential to help counter population growth, because they pave the way for a substantial reduction in serious global poverty. Clearly there are many factors that lead to increases in global population levels, but poverty in developing countries is a major one. A substantial decrease in global poverty, along with the cultural changes that would follow (such as improved education), could therefore contribute to a slowing of population growth towards stability.

Other direct measures, such as enforcing strict limits on birth rates, would be unacceptable attacks on people's important freedoms if serious steps were not taken first to address the root causes of population growth, such as poverty.

Local economies would be promoted

The promotion of local economies within the UK would achieve a number of aims, from strengthening local communities to creating more varied and vibrant high streets.

The various measures proposed, including increased corporation taxes, environmental taxes and stronger regulatory bodies, would help to regulate the impact of large companies on local communities and free up more money to invest in local economies. We could also take direct measures, including:

- Providing rate relief on the premises of a wider range of small retailers than is currently the case – for example independent newsagents and food, drink and tobacco shops. This relief could particularly focus on those threatened by out-of-town supermarkets or other developments by large organisations

- Introducing a local competition policy to limit the development of out-of-town superstores. Other countries such as France already have regulations that require special approval to be given for any proposed new store that is larger than 300 square metres. Local communities could be given the power to veto applications for new superstores or new chain stores from their high streets if they felt it was bad for the community

- Actively promoting more local markets, giving local producers the chance to trade on the high street and more 'pedestrian traffic' for local retailers.[11]

A further substantial measure to improve the situation would be to give local communities (through local authorities) greater power to make decisions about their quality of life, rather than such decisions being taken centrally. The Sustainable Communities Act, introduced in 2007 after vigorous campaigning from organisations including NEF, should provide a strong foundation to enable this to take place.[12]

We should also explore the possibilities for decentralising various areas of our lives. We currently rely on complex centralised systems to deliver some of our basic needs (such as food and energy), and this not only increases the complexity of the world for us but also makes us too heavily reliant on a central source, has a higher environmental impact than some decentralised alternatives, and means that we have little control over our supply of life's essentials. Some people are already starting to take control by producing some of these things for themselves – for example, various forms of microgeneration of energy. This is an area in which technological development can play an important role and be used for a positive purpose.

Aside from promoting local economies, many of these measures will also help us to shift to more sustainable, less energy-intensive lives.

Communities, society and political participation would be strengthened

Stronger communities are likely to emerge from the cumulative effects of the measures already suggested in this chapter. New conditions (including increased localisation, thriving high streets and planning to promote sustainable communities) and new attitudes (including a more relaxed view of time, more time for other people and a change of focus in life away from the pursuit of material wealth) would bring them into being almost as a matter of course.

In addition, the new system might encourage people to watch less television, by making people aware of its ability to isolate and induce lethargy, and by offering more opportunities to do other things. The development of stronger, more active communities could play a big part in this, as these could offer people the possibility of better social lives. Another step would be to establish more public meeting places in areas where they do not exist.

Another important ingredient in our new approach to economics would be to establish political arrangements that were more effective and democratic. These would include:

- A range of measures to rebalance power, including shifting it more from central to local government, ensuring that there is greater accountability from decision-makers and greater transparency in matters such as decision-making processes, and who holds which powers in office

- Measures to make the electoral system more responsive to people's needs, including replacing the first-past-the-post system (possibly with a system such as proportional representation (PR)), increasing the number of parties and candidates, and capping the amount an individual can donate to a party

- Creating the conditions to enable the public to become more involved in political decision-making, including requiring "all public bodies to meet a duty of public involvement in their decision and policy-making processes"[13] and establishing nationwide centres to give people access to clear, unbiased information and advice to help them lead well-informed lives and participate fully in society, including knowledge and advice on their political system and how to participate in it effectively.[14] These nationwide centres will be discussed in more detail in the 'Information Availability' section.

The cumulative effect of other recommendations in this chapter will also help to increase political participation, both of the formal type described above but also of the less formal types such as campaigning and community activism.

Mental freedom would be promoted

People need to have mental freedom – the capacity to make truly free choices, protect themselves from potentially harmful external influences and be truly self-determined. We cannot have real choice or be truly free until we have mental freedom, therefore it is almost as important for our well-being as physical freedom.

We are not born with mental freedom. We each need to be taught a number of thinking skills (or 'mental tools') in order to gain it. Mental tools are therefore some of the most important non-material resources people need in order to pursue the lives they want. A society geared towards well-being would recognise this, and would provide everyone with the mental tools needed to develop mental freedom, as well as the broader conditions required to maintain it. The tools themselves will be discussed later; in this section I would like to consider the conditions required in society to help people maintain their mental freedom.

An important principle here is that, unless it is strictly necessary, we should try to avoid interfering with society and people's lives with excessive regulation that attempts to 'protect' them from the various inputs and influences they might be subject to. Instead we should aim to equip people with the mental tools they need to make decisions for themselves. However, as we will see later in this chapter, we will still have to intervene in people's lives (through educating them) if we are to give them the mental tools needed to possess mental freedom – this point challenges the traditional idea that freedom is always about 'leaving people alone'.

Although we would want to limit some forms of regulation, it would be beneficial to establish a number of policies to protect people from certain inputs that could restrict their mental freedom, particularly in childhood, where their mental tools might not be sufficiently developed to enable them to act as truly self-determined agents. Two of the most obvious forms of biased input with undue influence and exposure in people's lives (and therefore requiring regulation) are consumerism and religion.

As regards consumerism, measures might include a ban on all forms of advertising to children under sixteen, and a law to ensure that any advertisement, promotion or campaign, from whatever source and in whatever medium, carries a prominent, standard label to show that it is attempting to communicate a message for a specific purpose. The labelling could include a summary of the source of the communication and the purpose, so there would be a small selection of standard labels, including 'commercial advertising campaign', 'government health campaign' and 'charity fundraising campaign'. It would be strictly regulated by an independent body.

With reference to religion, a ban on faith schools would give most children the chance to grow up without being instilled with a particular view of the world before they have had the chance to develop the mental tools and experience to think about and explore the topic for themselves.[15]

The availability of relevant information would improve

We need to help people to become better at dealing with the vast amount of information available to them in the world. This will involve equipping them with particular mental skills such as the ability to develop a strong sense of their own identity, as we shall discuss later.

However, the state can do other things to improve people's ability to interpret information. This does not involve restricting information, as access to it is an important freedom that must be preserved. Nor should it mean that the state acts as the public's only source of information, a scenario reminiscent of Orwell's 'Big Brother'. It can however help people to navigate through the wealth of information in the world and become better at using it.

Currently, Citizens' Advice Bureaux are useful sources of information on specific issues such as legal and money problems. Perhaps 'Information Advice Bureaux' could also be established: these would empower people with the skills to locate, use and manage information, as well as helping them gain access to the clear, unbiased information and advice they need to lead well-informed lives and participate fully in society. Their role might include helping people to:

- Locate the information they are seeking and develop the skills required to efficiently find information they may need in the future

- Understand and evaluate different sources of information

- Find reliable sources of information, or at least a selection of sources that they can confidently interpret and use

- Understand the principles of good research

- Develop the skills required to live in a world with so much information available

- Seek change, take action and get their voices heard, for example by providing advice on how they can become involved in their communities, or in political activity, or how they can participate in the political system.

There might also be a need for a separate, independent information service to provide people with clear, accessible and unbiased information on their relationship with the world and other people around them. This might include information on the following topics:

- Information to develop their 'global awareness' – including understanding of global issues, the links between issues, the 'causes' linking them and the nature and level of our global interconnection

- The influence they have as individuals on the rest of the world, including through the products they buy

- The influence the world has on their views and actions – where they obtain their information from and whether the nature of the source affects the message that is given.

Education would focus on life skills

In a society underpinned by the principles of new economics, the purpose of education would be to promote the well-being of individuals and society. It would provide people with some of the main non-material resources they need in order to live the lives they want. At present, we are in danger of teaching our children how to work and how to earn but not how to live [16] – or more specifically, we are not teaching them how to live happy, self-determined lives within the modern world.

An education system that taught children to do this would help them to develop skills in a range of areas, including 'the art of living well', the ability to be self-determined, the ability to think in philosophical and abstract ways and to develop social and emotional intelligence. The current education system – even taking into account areas such as citizenship education – does not adequately cover all these skills. In the second part of this chapter I will explore the basic skills that will be needed in some of these areas.

The need to promote well-being would be reflected not only in the subjects taught but in the whole approach to schooling. As NEF's *Well-Being Manifesto* says: "At its heart, education policy must acknowledge that the best way of enabling people to realise their potential is to value them for who they are rather than for their performance against targets. There is evidence to show that focusing heavily on testing can destroy learning, innovation, experimentation and original thinking." [17]

We should also rethink the role of education in life. Some of the skills I am describing are truly 'life skills' – skills that are not only useful throughout life but that can be developed throughout life. Perhaps it would therefore be beneficial to people's well-being to have the opportunity to develop or refresh them throughout their lives, not simply during their childhood. Under a new economy, some form of adult education allowance could therefore be provided to every individual, along with encouragement to make use of it – particularly in relation to developing the skills in the section below.

2. Updated Mental Tools

Now let us consider the mental tools we will need alongside the economic and social system outlined above. As I have said, we spend a greater proportion of our lives than ever before dealing with abstract things, and are subject to more influences than ever before, so it is now more important than ever for each of us to be better thinkers, simply to enable us to navigate our way effectively through the modern world and to live the lives we want. Thinking skills are also important for our well-being as they help to frame how we see the world and approach our lives. Policy-makers and the public alike need to be aware of this, as well as the fact that it is possible to teach such skills – it just requires a different focus of teaching.

Ideally, the skills below will help people to live better lives even in environments that are somewhat hostile to well-being, self-determination and human flourishing. Generally, however, no matter how empowered people are with these skills, they will need appropriate external conditions to truly flourish. Hence, a new economics underpinning society and a new toolkit of mental skills are complementary measures in the pursuit of human flourishing.

All the 'mental tools' in this section are included because they help to address some of the issues outlined in Part One. They also represent tools that are generally less common in the modern education system, although of course some schools are providing some of these skills to pupils.

They include skills in the 'art of living' together with thinking skills such as developing perspective and intellectual independence. The aim of some of the skills is to make people truly self-determined – giving them, as far as possible, control over themselves. This is an important form of freedom. Some of them will enable people to become 'everyday philosophers' – and whilst of course we do not need to reach the level of academics or professionals, we need to recognise the contribution that a basic level of these skills can make for a better life.

At this point it should be noted that each of us interacts with the world in a variety of ways, and not just through rational thought. Emotion, instinct and feelings also play a massive, and valuable, part in our lives. I am not suggesting that people are cold, rational 'calculating machines', or that we should aim to turn people into them through the provision of mental skills. As I've already suggested, the mental tools don't replace emotion, instinct or feelings, but work alongside them and can often help to give us greater insight on these aspects of our lives, including helping us to reveal our true feelings.

In Chapter 11 we will explore how we can develop some of these skills in our own lives now.

The mental tools

1. The art of living

This term covers a range of skills and attitudes that enable us to experience life in full and vibrant colour, to be in control of how we deal with life, and to live as we want. These skills are clearly fundamental to well-being.

a. How to live happily

Many people stumble along through life, with only occasional periods of real happiness. Over time, we each find ways of adjusting to life, some more successfully than others, but if happiness is such a desirable thing for human beings, why do we not teach people some of the skills that can help them to maintain a reasonably happy and well-adjusted view of the world? Some of these are listed below.

- *Understanding the nature of thought itself.* Learning what thoughts themselves actually are, and that it is possible for us to have some control over them. Also learning that it is possible to control the way we deal with them, which might include ignoring them if we wish. This skill can take some time to develop, but it can enable us to manage the way we perceive and approach the world. For example, if you know it is possible to train yourself to adopt a positive and optimistic attitude to life, this gives you at least some choice in how you approach and view your life, regardless of the external events you might go through during your lifetime. At the very least, this skill could teach us not to plague ourselves with imagined fears and worries.

- *Managing our relationship with certain abstract concepts.* For example, if we understand what 'expectations' are (arbitrary thoughts and ideas, sometimes self-imposed, sometimes imposed by others) and what it means to have them, we can take a lot of pressure off ourselves. Similarly, if we understand the nature of morality, we have a better chance of living in a way that is consistent with our values without punishing ourselves for failing to meet particular (sometimes impossible) standards. And realising that the idea of 'a purpose to life' is itself an abstract concept enables us to pursue the purpose we have chosen in life whilst appreciating that it is an arbitrary choice. It therefore enables us to focus on the journey in life, not just the destination, and also enables us to learn how to enjoy the journey.[18]

b. Developing and maintaining your personal identity

This is a central factor in developing a sense of well-being and in living the life we want.

Developing our personal identity is about knowing who we are, what we are about and what makes us happy. This is not always easy to do, as in a complex world sometimes even the most fundamental features of ourselves (e.g. our needs) can be obscured from our own view. Coaching in this area, combined with intellectual independence (to enable one to think about one's identity away from certain manipulative outside influences) would therefore be very useful for people.

Another element of developing one's personal identity is learning to be happy with it or accepting it, including accepting our natural features and realising that we are neither perfect nor imperfect – we are just ourselves. It also means seeing the best in ourselves and making the best of ourselves.

Developing this acceptance of your own identity contributes to the development of a final 'identity' skill – the ability to maintain this sense of identity throughout life. We need to be taught to trust ourselves and be comfortable with our judgements. This in turn enables us to live on our own terms, rather than feeling we have to follow others, for example in deciding the pace we want to live our lives at. We also need to be taught (or reminded) not to be afraid to be ourselves – in short, to let ourselves flourish.

A strong sense of identity gives you a secure place and point of view from which to evaluate and deal with the world around you – a set of judgements and instincts you can trust. It is also a place you can always return to in order to remind yourself of who you are, of your qualities and of what makes you happy. It is therefore a wonderful mental tool.

c. Deciding what you want in life

This is a skill closely linked to developing one's personal identity. It is about identifying what matters to us in life, what our priorities are and how we want to live. It is also about going through this process free from the influences and values of the society surrounding us, so that it more closely represents our genuine views.

If we have had the opportunity to develop a strong sense of personal identity reasonably early in life, it is likely to be easier to decide how we want to live and what we want. If however we are already immersed in the influences and complexity of society, we may need to be taught how to think about what we want out of life in order to reveal our identity rather than vice versa. This stage is included in the Three Step Programme in Chapter 11 to help you begin to make changes to your own life.

Before deciding what we want however, we will need to remove ourselves from the influences of the world, and to be able to do this we will need to develop a level of intellectual independence.

d. Awareness of subjective experience

This is the ability to appreciate the subjective experience of being a conscious creature and the sense of vitality and wonder this brings.

Many people use the term 'spiritual awareness' to describe this ability. I am not referring to any religious or mystical experience, but rather the ability to pause and reflect on the remarkable experience of being alive, including the feeling of existing, the fact that we exist alongside things of unimaginably larger and smaller size than ourselves, and that we are made from the same building-blocks as everything else.

Some of the other mental tools I have recommended (such as developing a certain form of perspective) will give us some of the information we need to think about these matters, but we also need to be encouraged to consider these big questions and to explore the experience of existing – in short, to find pleasure and fulfilment in contemplation.

This enables us to realise that we are a tiny part of something much larger, and puts the trials and tribulations of life into perspective. But it brings more than this: it can open our minds to completely new ways of thinking about our lives and our surroundings, and bring us adventure and stimulation throughout life. It can also help us to become wiser individuals.

Another important benefit of having this range of mental tools is to enable people to consider religious and other metaphysical ideas as part of an overall grounding in philosophy, and to be able to challenge them as they would be encouraged to challenge any other assumption. Thus, they would be able to form their own views on philosophical matters, without being indoctrinated by a particular point of view.

2. Perspective

Perspective is the ability to stand back and see a situation in a wider context. It is a mental tool that can be extremely useful when we are immersed in any form of complexity – from existing as a human being, to living our day-to-day lives, through to battling with a moral question.

People need to be taught the value of perspective in any situation, and how to develop it as a general thinking skill. To help people gain better lives in the modern world, we then need to help them to apply this skill to (at least) one situation – their own life in the modern world. To do this, we need to help people develop perspective across a particular range of topics, starting with the basic assumptions on which we base our views of reality, moving on to our situation within the universe and planet around us, through to our make-up as creatures and the systems and concepts we use to relate to each other and manage our lives. These topics include:

- The reality we live in, including philosophical questions such as 'what is reality?'

- Our situation, including our universe (its age, origins, size and scale, plus the place of our planet within it), and our planet (its terrain, the origin of life, what biological life consists of, and the diversity and extent of nature)

- Our species, including our characteristics as creatures (our biological and genetic make-up, our abilities and factors that influence our thinking and behaviour) and the variations in our circumstances on the planet (such as location, population levels and wealth)

- Human affairs, or how we manage our affairs as a species, including political systems, beliefs, values, cultures and the history of human affairs

- Our concepts. The abstract concepts that we use in our thinking and that inform our lives, including understanding what concepts actually are (including their parameters and how we can use them effectively), as well as how to understand specific concepts such as morality (what it means as a concept, what its parameters are and how we can use it effectively). This topic may seem to be less useful than the others, but it is an important new area in which people could be educated, and could bring major benefits. For example, it will help people to understand the structure of moral questions, the different ways we might respond to them, the assumptions that might underpin each response and the legitimacy of these assumptions. In short, it makes us better able to navigate around concepts such as morality, and better at using them.

In order to develop perspective on these topics (and others), people need to learn about them in a particular way. As we have noted in previous chapters, there is a massive amount of information and knowledge available to us in the world, and it is impossible for one person to have anything approaching a comprehensive knowledge, even of the restricted range of topics outlined above. We therefore need to teach people to develop knowledge of a topic in the same way as they would use a map to develop knowledge of a geographical area – rather than being stuck in the detail of one particular location, to see an overview of it and its parameters.

Maps are a useful metaphor for this way of learning and thinking. They work because they sacrifice detail (e.g. an exact description of the surroundings in a particular location, such as the colour of the flowers) in order to provide an overall perspective, and enable users to find their way around the terrain represented on the map. We need to do the same when learning about topics in order to gain perspective. In this way of learning, understanding the structure and parameters of a topic and how to navigate around it is just as important as understanding some of the detail, as this overview enables us to find our way around it and then seek further information on a particular area should we wish. There will need to be detail within each topic area but it will need to focus on appropriate and useful sub-topics and be at a level that is consistent with the overall purpose of the 'map' – too much detail will make the 'map' too complex to use, and too little will also limit its usefulness.

Even concepts such as morality have parameters and structure that people can learn about, in order to help them find their way around specific moral views and arguments better.

Perspective on one's life in the great scheme of things can provide benefits for our philosophical well-being and help us navigate our way through life more easily.

If we know little about our situation in the world, our history, culture, concepts and other aspects of life, then our awareness of life will be as restricted as our view of the world might be if we were sitting in the middle of a forest without a map. Our path through life will therefore be as random and uninformed as our path through the forest would be, and we would have little knowledge to give us any comfort about our place within the 'bigger picture'. The solution in both situations is the same – we need to 'lift ourselves above' the position we find ourselves in, and gain perspective on it. We do this by increasing our knowledge of certain aspects of the world around us, using a map.

I therefore suggest that perspective can help us to achieve two things that will contribute to the ultimate aim of living happier and more fulfilled lives. Firstly:

- It can help us to understand 'where we are' in the broadest possible sense – to form a conception of the 'big picture' we live within. This will be beneficial for us in a number of ways, the simplest being that having a picture of 'where we are' tends to reduce our anxiety and give us a certain sense of calm in our lives. For example, if one can picture one's own life within the context of the larger universe and history itself, one emerges with a sense that one is reasonably insignificant yet extraordinarily lucky to have the chance to experience life. This can provide one with a range of positive thoughts to carry through daily life, including a sense of comfort that, whatever the trials and tribulations of one's own life, we are part of something much bigger. It can also provide an injection of energy, enthusiasm and wonder into every day of being alive. It is also a form of wisdom, as among many other things, it enables us to understand ourselves better, react in a more balanced way to the highs and lows of life and view other people in a more understanding way.

- A second benefit of perspective is that it can help us to better understand various major aspects of our lives and the world. As a consequence, it can help us to navigate our way through life more easily, both on large questions and everyday ones. For example, it can help us to consider big questions such as how we should live and what path to pursue in our lives. It can also aid our decision-making about more detailed, everyday issues such as moral questions ('how should I behave in this situation?').

This method of thinking could be particularly useful and appropriate in the modern world, given the increasingly high levels of complexity and accumulated knowledge that surround each of us, and the increased difficulty of navigating this. It means we don't have to know everything in order to live well-informed lives.

The manifold disadvantages of not possessing perspective can be taken to be the reverse of each of the points above – for example, having an unrealistic view of the world or your own situation as a creature, getting stressed or confused by the apparent complexity of the world and making poor decisions in life.

3. Intellectual independence

In this book there have been many examples of people adopting attitudes and assumptions from the world around them without challenging them. Intellectual independence enables people to challenge the inputs they are receiving and any overarching assumptions in their society. It includes critical thinking skills, but is more than this. It is the ability to be self-determined, to make decisions and choices for ourselves without being influenced by external forces that may seek to manipulate us. It enables us to live life on our own terms.

Part of this skill is being aware of our inputs – in other words, understanding the sources of the messages we receive and assessing their reliability and potential biases. It also includes other thinking skills such as dealing with the complexity of information around us – being able to assess what information is relevant, how to find it and how to reach a balanced judgement on it.

Finally, it involves a sense of self-determination and courage – recognising that one can be in control of one's own life, and having the courage to live in accordance with one's values, even if these are not consistent with the political or social norm. A more detailed list of the tools of intellectual independence is provided in the appendix of this book.

4. Abstract thinking skills

Abstract thinking skills underpin the other mental skills discussed in this chapter, and they also need to be taught. They can be as important as knowledge itself, and teaching should focus as much on developing them. Teaching people to think for themselves will help them to find the knowledge they need in a given situation.

These skills include understanding that there are different ways of managing one's thinking and thoughts, and how different thinking techniques can help in different circumstances. They also include developing a basic philosophical understanding of what 'concepts' actually are, and understanding the concepts we most commonly use, such as morality. Understanding morality better would help us to become more effective moral agents, and more able to deal with the complexities and challenges of living with moral values – skills that are important for our ability to lead lives that are sustainable and socially just as well as happy and fulfilling.

Overall, these abstract thinking skills would save us time, energy and stress, and help us to make better judgements. Furthermore, they would help us to develop a level of 'intellectual agility' that could give us pleasure and would make us better equipped to achieve any goals we had set ourselves in life. See the appendix for a more detailed list of useful abstract thinking skills.

5. Other areas of knowledge

Other areas of knowledge that need to be promoted more in society include:

- Practical knowledge – an understanding of the basic processes that we are part of, including energy supply, food supply, clothing manufacture and supply, and media sources. This would help to reduce the complexity of the modern world for us and enable us to make better choices and better judgements about how we want to live.

- Sustainability literacy – including understanding the effects we have on the planet and on other people, and what we can do to live in a sustainable way. A full sustainability literacy programme would need to include topics such as ethics and seeing our situation as individuals in a wider context.

- Political awareness – not just awareness of issues in current affairs, but an understanding of the political system itself and how to participate in it most effectively.

How the tools could be delivered

The main delivery vehicle for these skills would of course be the education system, in order to ensure that everyone is given the opportunity to develop the skills and have access to the information they need. The introduction of these skills would be part of the rebalancing of the education system, including a revised view of what education is for, the skills people need in life and when they should be provided.

The state should further promote the development of these skills by establishing national and local institutions to provide opportunities to reflect on life, learn new thinking skills and gain support in using them. They could also help to promote the benefits of these skills. They could develop facilities such as an Ethics Support Service to help people consider what values are, what their values are, how to put them into practice and how to live effectively and happily with them. Opportunities for this self-development should be open to all, throughout life.

There is also considerable potential for institutions such as 'non-religious churches'* to bring people together and fulfil some of the useful functions that currently only appear to be served by religious groups, but to do so without invoking any god or supernatural belief. These functions include regular reflection on ethical matters, and reflection to gain perspective on the bigger issues in life.

Independent initiatives are also being developed specifically to deliver the skills mentioned in this section. One proposal for such a scheme is called 'just think...' (JT). It is an informal, self-taught course undertaken by small local groups of eight to ten people, each with a self-appointed leader or facilitator. It would provide participants with a model for independent, well-informed thinking on particular topics (initially, their ethical values and their view of 'quality of life') and give them information, the opportunity for reflection and advice and support in helping them make changes to their lives.

JT is by no means a panacea, but it is designed to be an accessible starting point, looking at two important areas of life, from which people can begin to develop their intellectual independence and values awareness and expand the use of these into other areas of their lives. It and other such similar schemes could be extended to promote the development of these skills across all areas of life – effectively a guide to living well in the modern world. For more information on the scheme, visit www.justthink.org.uk. There is also considerable potential for many other schemes to provide thinking skills.

---

* For more information on this idea, download the free report 'The Joy of Sects' from http://www.changestar.co.uk/thinking_reports.htm.

Conclusion

The recommendations set out in this chapter are interconnected and form a unified approach to seeking a better world. This can only be achieved if we take big steps to address the causes of our problems rather than smaller steps to temporarily alleviate the symptoms.

This vision of a better society was neatly summarised by the sustainable development charity Forum for the Future in 2005:

> Everyone's human rights and basic needs are met. Everyone has access to good food, water, shelter, and sustainable sources of energy at reasonable cost. People's health is protected by creating safe, clean and pleasant environments, as well as health services that prioritise the prevention of illness while providing proper care for the sick. People live without fear of personal violence from crime or persecution on account of their personal beliefs, race, gender or sexuality.
>
> The economic system serves people and the environment. It is market-based to ensure innovation and efficiency, but rigorously regulated to secure social and environmental benefits as well as economic benefits. Where practical, local needs are met locally. The ambition of politicians and community leaders is to ensure the highest possible quality of life within the operating limits of the natural world. Everyone has access to the skills, knowledge and information needed to enable them to play a full part in society, and everyone has the opportunity to undertake satisfying work in a diverse economy. The value of unpaid work is recognised, while payments for work are fair and fairly distributed.
>
> Society is founded on democracy, tolerance and diversity. All sections of the community are empowered to participate in decision-making. Opportunities for culture, leisure and recreation are readily available to all, and places, spaces and objects combine meaning and beauty with utility. Settlements are 'human' in scale and form. Ethnic and cultural diversity and local distinctiveness are valued and protected.
>
> The Earth is nurtured as a single community, bound together with independent relationships. Our life-support systems are afforded the highest political priority. Resources are used ultra-efficiently, waste is minimised by closing cycles and pollution is limited to levels which natural systems can cope with without damage. The diversity of nature is valued and protected, regardless of its usefulness to humankind.[19]

The problems we currently face may seem substantial and the dominance of neoliberal capitalism unchallengeable, but history suggests that the ideas and systems that govern us are never fixed – there will always be changes and new ideas. Change comes when people decide that they are motivated enough by a particular issue to get up and take action. We do not have to accept what we have at the moment, so if we care about it enough, let us do something about it.

Chapter 11

How can we change our own lives?

Some of the social changes discussed in the previous chapter would take time to achieve and would require a concerted effort from everyone – politicians, organisations and individuals. In the meantime there are things we can do now to make our own lives better.

The steps we can take can be divided into two broad categories: mental and practical. The mental steps involve us teaching ourselves to develop some of the mental skills discussed in Chapter 10, so that we can change the way we see the world or approach life. The practical steps include actions we can take to address some of the issues raised in Part One.

This is not intended as a detailed self-help book, so I aim only to provide initial pointers and recommendations. At the end of the book I have provided a number of links and references to organisations and materials that offer the opportunity to explore issues in more detail. Before we consider what we can each do in relation to the problems identified in Part One, here are some general steps we can take.

Seeking social and global change

One of the most important things we can do as individuals in response to the findings of this book is to take action to seek the changes suggested in the previous chapter. This might take the form of campaigning, lobbying MPs, writing to international institutions, or a range of other steps. Here is a brief list of the actions that we can each take to push forward the broader changes set out there.

- **Find out more about the issues.** Read some of the relevant magazines and books, and become more familiar with the movement for change. This will enable you to feel part of something bigger, find out where your particular interests lie and identify the areas to which you want to devote your time.

- **Become involved in organisations that are seeking broad economic change.** It is worthwhile joining or contacting organisations with a broad perspective, such as the New Economics Foundation, as this will enable you to learn more about the issues, meet others and find ways to make your contribution as effective as possible.

- **Get involved in organisations campaigning on individual issues.** There are also a number of campaign groups seeking change on individual issues that will each help to achieve our overall vision of a better future. One should however be careful to check whether all their work and policies are consistent with the general vision of a new economics – for example, a number of development organisations seem happy not to challenge the notion of consumerism.

- **Write to politicians.** Write to your local MP and other influential political figures about the issues raised in this book, and ask them what they are doing about them. Suggest that they read this book.

- **Raise these issues in public.** Talk to people about the issues raised in this book, not in an evangelising way, but simply seeing what others think about them. If they sound interested, suggest that they read the book. Very few people get to consider the 'bigger picture' behind their lives or global issues, so simply ensuring that these ideas become part of everyday conversation is an important contribution to moving them forward.

- **Do your bit.** I have tried to provide a broad idea of what a more sustainable and just world would look like. It is also reasonably clear what sort of behaviour it would require from us as individuals to gain and sustain this world. For example, living within the resources of one planet (reducing your consumption of natural resources and your levels of waste) and living in a socially just way (which includes redistributing some resources to the extremely poor and avoiding actions that exploit others). We should therefore each live in a way that is consistent with this overall vision even if others have not yet realised that they need to do so.

I have provided pointers to some useful organisations and resources to help you in the 'Further Reading and Links' section at the end of the book.

Mental skills: the three-step programme

As I have said, one of the major things we can do to improve our lives is to change the way we think about ourselves and the world around us. I will not attempt to cover every mental skill we discussed earlier, as the development of some of them requires a training and support structure. But we can consider the skills we can each develop without much external coaching or teaching.

Firstly I'd like to summarise some of the steps we can take to develop these simple mental skills. I've presented these as a Three-Step Programme that could be undertaken before embarking on the detailed practical actions recommended later in this chapter, as most of them make use of these steps. The programme represents a good starting point to develop the mental skills and take the steps needed to create a better life in the modern world.

Step 1. Develop a broad perspective and use it in daily life

There are many uses of the thinking skill of seeking perspective, and each is important. But perhaps the most immediate thing we can do is to gain perspective on our situation as individuals in the great scheme of things, and consider what consequences it has for the way we think about and approach life. We can then live day-to-day life with this perspective in the back of our minds, as a piece of wisdom that reminds us of various things, including the fact that we each only get a few years of life, with no distinct purpose to them and that we should live them in the way we feel is right. And that any pressures on us or expectations of us telling us how we should live or what we should do have ultimately been constructed by our society, so we can judge each on its merits and choose to ignore it if we please. We will also be able to take control of the way we see and experience the world, and consequently experience life in a calm, clear and happy way.

A quick way to gain this perspective is to allocate a period of time (perhaps a weekend) in which to withdraw from the modern world and the consumerist system. Take yourself away from distractions such as television, and perhaps even remove yourself from contact with other people. During this time, try to do two things:

(a) **Develop perspective about your life and situation.** Pick some topic areas from the list recommended as part of the 'Perspective' mental tool in Chapter 10. You should at least look at 'Our Situation' and 'Our Species', as they provide some basic context. You can choose how much information to take in – remember you can add to your stock of knowledge on an ongoing basis after this weekend – but the idea is to build some initial perspective on your position as an individual.

You can choose how to develop perspective on these topics, but it may be most effective to use a mixture of a little research and putting yourself into situations that bring this learning to life and make it real for you. For example, as part of the 'Our Situation' section, you could go out to the countryside and appreciate nature – from large scale (landscapes, skies and trees etc.) through to small (taking the time to look below a stone or within the grass) and also read about our planet and the life on it. You could also look up to the sky at night through some binoculars, having read about the universe and our place in it. Both these situations can bring some perspective even without being accompanied by much learning, as they make us escape from modern life.

While you are looking at these topics, think about your own position and life in relation to them. For example, what conclusions can you draw about these things from looking at the stars and learning about the universe?

(b) **Consider what implications this perspective has for your life and how you choose to see things.** One conclusion you might reach is that we ourselves are part of nature and therefore part of the ebb and flow of events that nature goes through over time – a thought that may make you feel considerably calmer. Be prepared to challenge your assumptions about life and the way you live it. For example, with perspective you may find it hard to justify why you get anxious about certain elements of everyday life, given the great scheme of things. If you can't justify having this anxiety in the face of perspective, just drop the old thinking and feel calmer – even if it feels strange to do so!

Needless to say, some of the conclusions you reach may be considerably different from your previous views, but learn to trust the views you gain from perspective, perhaps by having another 'perspective weekend' a few weeks later and realising that the conclusions of the first have not gone away. The extent to which you trust these views and implement them in your life will be the extent to which you are living authentically.

Before you resume your life at the end of this time, resolve to incorporate this perspective and your conclusions into your life and decide how you will do so, perhaps through a ten-minute session of reflection each day. It is important to plan the specifics of how you will put this into action, as once you are back in the rush of modern life your experience of the weekend will feel weaker. Remember how it feels when all the great resolutions you made whilst on a holiday vanish into thin air when you arrive home? Its a similar situation – and one that can be overcome with a bit of planning and determination.

This perspective is something that can be developed and built over a lifetime, therefore even giving a whole weekend to it is clearly just a very basic starting point, but at least it is a starting point. It may therefore be worth resolving, as an investment in yourself, to continue to build your learning about your situation as an individual human being.

Having gained this initial perspective, you can undertake a second useful activity.

Step 2. Consider what you want in life

A central feature of making our mental lives better is to identify the lives we really want. Currently, as we have seen, the complexity and influences of modern society can obscure our view of this. So we need to strip away these layers before we consider what we want in life. This will not only reveal what we really want but also help us to remember and appreciate our real identities.

This task should therefore involve a similar process to developing perspective. You should temporarily remove yourself from the modern world to think through the question. This process could therefore be undertaken on the same weekend as the 'perspective weekend' in the previous point, but the two things are a lot to cram into one short space of time. It would be better to allocate another weekend or day to considering what you want out of life.

The first stage in this process will be to go through the conclusions you reached from developing your perspective, as this will help you to see beyond your current situation. Then in the light of this perspective, start trying to identify some of the things that are important to you in life. These might include love, friendship, money, children, ethical values, possessions etc.

You should then consider whether some of these things really are important to you or are the result of external influences. Look back through your life and identify the various influences that have affected you (from childhood onwards, through to day-to-day influences in the present), where they have come from and where you feel they may have led you away from the things that really matter to you. For example, if you attach great importance to your career, is this partly because of an external influence telling you that it is important in order to earn as much as possible? And has this suppressed other things you value such as time with your family? As you reach the end of this process of stripping away the external influences you may emerge with new priorities in life or simply rebalance your existing ones.

Once you have developed a list of your genuine priorities, think about whether you are currently living in line with them. Where you are not, think about how your life could be adjusted to do so. For example, has your life become too geared towards chasing some of the goals set by consumerism and neoliberal economic thinking? Could it be rebalanced towards other things that genuinely make you happy, and become better as a result?

This process will hopefully be a real pleasure, as you produce a range of ideas that energise and excite you. These might range from the big ('let's run away to a cottage in Italy') to the small ('I'll ask for a four-day week and spend more time with my family') – that all energise and excite you. As the ideas flow, begin to balance them and assess their feasibility. Some may simply be impossible given your current situation and one benefit of perspective is the ability to accept your situation and make the most of it. Some may be impractical at the moment but could be a vision for the longer-term future. Others may involve breaking through barriers that you originally thought were there but that are in fact simply the product of arbitrary influences and expectations of society, such as the need to earn as much money as possible. And it is these 'phantom barriers' that we should all develop the courage and strength of mind to break through.

A happy path in life therefore involves both identifying where the real parameters in your situation are and accepting them, and also identifying apparent barriers that can actually be broken through.

Another important result that is likely to emerge from this process is that you will develop a stronger sense of your own identity, including who you are and what you want from life. It might put you back in touch with some aspects of yourself that you had forgotten. And once you have a stronger sense of your identity, you can learn to accept it and be happy with it. This is what you are and these are the things you genuinely want, so trust your judgement on these things.

This increased sense of identity also includes accepting your abilities, appearance and every other natural aspect of yourself. You are neither perfect nor imperfect – you are just you. Anything that would have you believe otherwise is an arbitrary judgement by external influences and the key point of developing a strong sense of identity is to put a barrier between yourself and external views of what you should be.

As I have said, the erection of this barrier gives you a secure place from which to evaluate and deal with the world around you and to choose which influences you want to let in and listen to. Whatever the complexity and influences in the world, a strong sense of (and happiness with) your identity will be a central factor in helping you to live a happy, self-determined life.

Step 3. Pursue the life you want whilst defending yourself against external influences

Once you have identified what matters to you and resolved to live an authentic life, you will find that you are faced with regular challenges to your thinking, such as external sources attempting to influence you or a lack of support (perhaps even ridicule or hostility) for your decision to go against the cultural norm. As we have seen, some of these challenges will stem from the complexity of the world and the influences of neoliberal capitalism and consumerism.

There are a range of mental tools that can assist you in this constant battle, and many are presented in Chapter 10. Later, in the 'Steps for Specific Problems' section, I will provide examples of how they can be applied to the problems identified in Part One, but here are some general principles:

- **Exercise intellectual independence.** Two important mental tools to use in this process are:

  Critical thinking, in which you get into the habit of questioning all the external messages you receive, and evaluate whether the sources are reliable, what the purpose of the message is and whether it is something to be digested or ignored.

Protecting your personal identity by developing a strong sense of who you are and what matters to you, trusting it and resisting suggestions from external sources that you should change yourself or your thinking. These influences should not necessarily prevent you from developing yourself or changing your thinking on particular matters, but before you do so you should think the issue through for yourself, consult reliable sources and conclude whether it would be of genuine benefit to you.

- **Find support.** It is always easier to maintain your direction if you have access to a support network of like-minded people or even just access to forums and information that are sympathetic to your views and aims. So try to find organisations, groups and links that represent your views and either get involved or keep in touch with them. Some of the links provided at the end of the book may be useful starting points. If friends and others in your social circle feel as you do, an ideal support network can develop.

- **Be happy.** Using a combination of the factors discussed above, including perspective, intellectual independence and a strong personal sense of identity, you can develop a sense of calm and happiness – a feeling that, whatever the world throws at you, you have the wisdom to see it in context and maintain a sense of proportion.

The main point to take from this section is to live your life your way, and to be happy doing so. It sounds simple, but if you are immersed in the modern world with all its complexity and influences, it can require an effort to identify what 'your way' is, plus courage and mental strength to follow it and to be happy with your identity. The steps outlined above may be a useful introduction to this way of thinking.

Steps for specific problems

Let us now discuss how you might respond to each of the problems outlined in Part One. Some of the recommendations may seem fairly obvious, but they are often things we can overlook as we rush through our busy lives, and often the simplest things have the most profound effect, for example introducing yourself to your neighbours when you move somewhere new. Others are about breaking down barriers, some of which are arbitrary social barriers and others are those we might have created for ourselves.

Our lives are too rushed

- **Live life at your own pace.** Choose for yourself the pace at which you want to live, and whether you want to be busy or not. This may mean standing back from the rush of modern life and experiencing what it is like to live more slowly, then deciding whether you like it. If not, you can resume your fast life, but at least you will have made an informed choice.

  This ultimately goes back to one of the main points discussed earlier in this chapter. You need to decide what matters to you in your life and how you want to live it, and then have the courage to seek this sort of life. Having drawn some conclusions, you may decide that you want to adjust your current way of living. For example, you may decide that your priorities are not about earning as much as possible, but about balancing a fulfilling work-life with your family, and enjoying the experience of life. You might therefore ask to work fewer hours or even seek a different job that brings less pressure and intensity. Or you might decide that you want less quantity but more quality in your social activities.

- **Ignore the rushers.** There will always be people who choose to live rushed and stressed lives, and there will also be those who do not have the courage or ability to live more slowly even though they want to. But if you have chosen not to live this kind of life, then don't make yourself anxious by comparing yourself to these people. Be happy with your identity and choices, live at your own pace and ignore any pangs of guilt, or the temptation to compare yourself with others, or any sense of missed opportunity when you see other people striving endlessly or living busier lives than you.

- **Don't be a slave to time.** Although we may all sometimes have to conform to accepted ideas of time (for example, arriving at meetings at an agreed hour), we do not have to conform to the standard modern view of how to use our time, i.e. that it is a resource that we must use as efficiently as possible. This conception of time leads to the problems we discussed in Chapter 1, as well as various forms of anxiety (such as worrying that we are wasting time) and regret (e.g. that 'the years are slipping away') that can cast a negative pall over our lives.

Whatever goals we might decide to seek in life, we should try to enjoy the journey as well, by simply enjoying the experience of being alive, and the quality of our time, not just the quantity. How we judge this quality will depend on our individual views of what matters in life. So decide what matters to you and then decide how your time should be used; do not let the arbitrary modern view of time influence you or ruin your life. Even if you do decide that you like being busy, regularly take a little time to 'enjoy the journey' and take in the experience of living.

- **Have some daily reflection time.** No matter how busy your life is, you can afford to give yourself at least ten minutes each day to sit quietly without disturbance, close your eyes, relax and remove yourself from the rush. You might choose to banish all thoughts until you develop a sense of calm, as in meditation, or to stand back from your life and see it in greater perspective. Either way, take some time each day to withdraw from the world and remind yourself that your life is part of something much bigger, that your thoughts are just abstract ideas and that you can control your response to the world. Many people find that activities such as meditation, yoga or walking in the countryside can help this process, but choose the way that suits you best. This provides a daily top-up of perspective that is useful in its own right and also takes you off the treadmill for a short period, reminding you of a different way of using your time.

- **Say no.** Many of us find it difficult to refuse requests for our time, whether at work or socially. As a consequence, we become busier and busier. We should assign greater importance to our own time, realise that it is our choice as to how we use it, and that we do not have to exist as machines that must agree to every demand others make of us.

- **Throw away your alarm-clock.** This recommendation is made by Tom Hodgkinson in *How to be Idle*, and I cannot resist including it. The alarm-clock provides a nice metaphor for the way in which we have become slaves to other people's idea of time – specifically those with their own ideas of what is good for us or society. Although we may have to get up at a particular time to go to work, the experience of being woken up by the shriek of the alarm-clock is unpleasant, and feels as though we are being woken by those who want to control us, rather than in the way we would choose ourselves. Surprisingly enough, we can control our own waking patterns naturally, with considerable accuracy. Some people find that they can wake naturally at the time they need to without using an alarm-clock, with only a few days of training.

Our natural spaces are under threat

- **Make use of our natural spaces.** One of the most effective ways of showing how much we value our natural spaces is for us to use them. Visit and enjoy them, and try to do so in ways that minimise your impact on their tranquillity – for example, try not to drive if possible.

- **Do not add an unnecessary burden on them.** Think about the knock-on effects of your personal actions on our natural spaces, and do not place unnecessary additional burden on them. Limit the demand for new house building through actions such as not buying a second home. Limit the demand for new infrastructure: for example, flying less will reduce demand for airport expansion. And limit the demand for new roads through actions such as driving less.

Shopping is hell

- **Shop locally.** Even if you cannot give up supermarket shopping entirely, shop locally as much as you can. See it as being about more than just acquiring goods: it is also an opportunity to build social networks, enjoy your local area and find out about what is going on locally. Also consider buying directly from producers, such as from farm shops or local vegetable box schemes.

- **Keep money in the local economy.** 'Keeping it local' is not simply about buying your groceries from the local shops, but also using local producers and services and trying to make a contribution to the local economy. Look to local producers or services before you go further afield or to national chains, whether for car repairs, buying clothes, using cafés or DVD rentals. Encourage shops to stock locally produced goods.

- **Set up a local distribution scheme.** Join with others and set up a group that buys staple food items in bulk from local suppliers such as health food shops. This enables group members to get substantial discounts on their food and to form a co-operative local venture.

- **Grow your own.** This is the ultimate form of localisation. Growing your own produce is not only an effective way to reduce your reliance on supermarkets, but is also a source of great pleasure. It is an opportunity to slow down, to become immersed in something, to be close to nature and to produce food with the minimum level of environmental impact. If you don't have a garden, you can grow produce on a small scale (even in window-boxes) or obtain an allotment for a very low annual fee – contact your local council for details.

- **Contribute some capital to a different type of local economy.** Economies do not have to use money as the form of capital. As we have seen, LETS schemes provide a marketplace for people to offer skills, services and goods without money changing hands. Currencies are agreed by the group, and may take various forms. In some groups an hour of everyone's time might be worth the same amount, but in others some services might be valued more highly than others. The focus away from money can make these schemes more inclusive, and they can also represent a good way to get to know people in your area and build networks of co-operation.

We're losing our communities

- **Meet your neighbours.** This may seem a rather obvious point, but many of us do not bother to do it. When you move somewhere new or when you see new neighbours moving in, go round and introduce yourself. Invite them round. It is also a nice idea to organise a get-together for the residents of your street from time to time – for no better reason than to meet and catch up with each other.

- **Help your neighbours and ask for their help.** Offering and asking for help is a useful way of strengthening community ties and building a sense that neighbours can count on each other, whether it is offering to do their shopping, some DIY, or to keep an eye on their home when they are on holiday. And asking for help is an equally useful way to kick off this social process, especially as although almost everyone is willing to give help, very few people are willing to ask for it.[1]

- **Talk to people.** Break down the social barriers that isolate us from each other by changing your attitude about your relationships with strangers. When out and about in your local community, start conversations with people. Treat your local community as a community – a public place where you meet people and converse. You share things in common with those who live locally to you – why not break down the barriers and strike up conversation? Instigating a conversation in this way may feel slightly odd at first, but that is simply because social convention says it is so. Wouldn't it make us feel truly connected with other people and where we live if we knew that there were none of these awkward and socially isolating conventions in place?

- **Start a social group.** There are often few opportunities for local communities to get together, except for particular groups such as churches and sports clubs. Why not organise a regular evening in a local venue where everyone is invited simply to socialise, meet each other and share news? Although the main purpose of these events is simply to get people together, they have the potential to produce useful spin-offs such as other social events, new community schemes, friendships and ideas to help people. All you need to do is find a venue, set a date and publicise it, and people will come! For further ideas on how to set up an event like this (including template publicity posters) go to www.changestar.co.uk/gs_home.htm.

- **Volunteer or participate in community groups.** In many communities there is a huge array of opportunities to volunteer or get involved in groups. These include nature conservation, helping the elderly and joining local campaign groups for national organisations. One popular new community-led scheme that has emerged in recent years is the Transition Towns initiative, in which members of a community come together to explore how that community can respond to the challenges and opportunities presented by peak oil and climate change. See www.transitiontowns.org for more details.

Volunteering opportunities may not be advertised in the most obvious places, but an enquiry at your local Community Service Volunteers bureau (www.csv.org.uk) or a flick through the Yellow Pages will yield results. Timebanks (www.timebank.org.uk), which could be regarded as an updated version of the LETS scheme, also offer a way for you to donate your time to a whole host of different projects, whether local or beyond. Aside from these 'official' routes, it is also useful to see your time as a resource that could be offered to anyone, anywhere in your community, so if there is a shop, business, person or cause you would like to give some time to, why not just approach them?

- **Unplug your television.** Better still, unplug it and turn it to face the wall! I do not want to suggest that watching television is a terrible thing. But it does have the ability to incapacitate us and prevent us from doing other things. So, make it harder for yourself to watch it, and remove it as the focal point of your living-room.

Consumerism dominates everything

- **Exercise intellectual independence.** Be aware of how consumerism touches your life and when people or organisations are trying to manipulate you. Seek to defend yourself from unwanted external pressures. One effective way to do this is to regard advertising as a form of mental pollution and simply ignore it – don't let it affect you or take up any of your time or brain space.

Avoidance is one strategy, but it is also important to build up the intellectual independence to deal with consumerism. When you receive any message, whether it is in a social conversation, at work, in a newspaper, or on television, consider the source it came from and whether it might have a particular agenda. Decide whether you can trust it and whether you should make any allowances for it in your interpretation of the message. You can then choose whether the message is to be digested or ignored. As we have seen, this doesn't simply refer to specific messages such as advertisements but even broader cultural or social beliefs such as the importance of striving for greater material wealth.

- **Consume less, live more.** Live the life you want, not the one that others would like you to lead. For many of us, a life of consumerism and constantly striving to gain further material wealth is not the one we would choose upon honest reflection. Many of us will find that reducing our levels of consumption, caring less about materialism and refocusing our attention and time towards things that really matter to us will eliminate a lot of problems in our lives and give us a great deal more satisfaction, whilst also leading to a more sustainable and fair future for all.

We're not involved in politics

- **Become involved.** The problems outlined in Chapter 6 specifically refer to the decline in formal voting and the unsuitability of the current electoral system. This issue will only be resolved through political change, and there are few actions that can be taken at the individual level to achieve this, other than campaigning for electoral reform.

- **Become informed.** Find out more about political issues, the range of parties that could represent you, the political system itself and how to participate in it most effectively.

The world is too large and too complex

- **Trust your identity.** Perhaps the most important recommendation for individual action to manage the complexity of the world is to go through the Three-Step Programme, particularly Step 2, the process of identifying the things that are important to you and becoming self-determined and happy with your identity. This self-determination will give you a reasonable 'filter' for the complexity in the modern world, enabling you to identify what information and messages are relevant to you and to ignore the rest, without feeling overwhelmed by information or options. Essentially, it enables you to act as the subject (moulding the world to your purposes) rather than the object (with the world moulding you). This is not to suggest that once you have identified the things that matter to you, you should close yourself to the possibility of expanding your horizons further, but rather that a sense of identity provides you with a 'complexity filter'.

- **Exercise intellectual independence.** To overcome the variety of influences on your life, employ the tools of intellectual independence recommended under 'Consumerism dominates everything' above.

- **Find some trusted sources of information.** No source of information is completely unbiased, but it is possible to build a selection of trusted sources that can summarise and filter some of the complexity in the world for you. By finding these sources and understanding their biases, you can build a useful resource to help you deal with the complexity of the world on an ongoing basis. These may include newspapers, websites and other information resources. It may be useful to choose a selection of media with different points of view, to help you reach your own conclusions.

- **Build your knowledge of relevant topics.** If you have been through the process of reviewing the things that matter to you in life, you will have built a clearer idea of your identity and will therefore have a better understanding of the topics of interest to you. You will also have briefly explored some that can contribute to the development of perspective.

  Aim to build your knowledge in these combined areas on an ongoing basis – not necessarily through an exhaustive and formal study plan, but simply through an awareness that learning more about these areas could make life easier, happier and more fulfilling. A good set of topics to build knowledge on initially are those that specifically interest you, plus those discussed in the 'Perspective' mental tool in Chapter 10. An efficient way to build knowledge on these topics would be through developing 'perspective' on them, as discussed in Chapter 10, by trying to get an overview of the territory and key points of a subject rather than struggling through massive detail (unless of course you want this detail).

- **Live a less complex life.** One way to reduce complexity in your life is to reduce your radius of impact on the world. For example, buying your food locally and buying local produce where possible will reduce the range of processes, transactions and people involved in supplying your food.

  In general, the simpler and more local you can make your life, the smaller your radius of impact is likely to be and therefore the less complexity you will find. Consuming less will therefore also reduce your radius of impact.

- **Have some daily reflection time.** This point was discussed under 'Our lives are too rushed' above.

- **Learn and practice thinking skills.** In Chapter 7 I suggested that we lack certain thinking skills, and in Chapter 10 I recommended ways in which they could be promoted and taught to both children and adults. You can also learn some basic thinking skills on your own, including the following:

  Moving between detailed arguments and broader assumptions. Identify the assumptions and views behind your position on a particular question (e.g. 'fox-hunting is wrong'), and trace these back to your most basic assumptions about the world (e.g. 'killing animals is wrong'). This process of identifying our most basic beliefs and assumptions might lead us to question the consistency of our views on other more detailed matters (e.g. if we believe killing animals is wrong, should we be eating meat?). It also enables us to challenge some of our most basic assumptions and views, and understand at what point other people's assumptions and views differ from ours.

  Identifying the territory of a subject. Seek a broad understanding of a topic and its parameters first of all, rather than jumping into just one area of detail within it (e.g. understanding the spectrum of possible roles of the state, from anarchism to totalitarianism, and the variety of possibilities that could lie in between them).

  Besides learning these specific skills, as a general rule it is always worthwhile to learn new thinking skills. There are many books and courses available that teach a range of thinking skills.

People aren't flourishing

- **Trust your identity.** As with some of the sections above, perhaps the most important recommendation for individual action to protect your identity is to go through the Three-Step Programme, and in particular Step 2 – the process of identifying the things that are important to you and developing a stronger sense of your own identity.

  The ability to evaluate and deal with the world from a secure place (your own sense of identity) means that when others suggest that you need to develop yourself in particular areas, you have the strength and intellectual independence to decide whether to absorb or reject these external influences.

It also enables you to set your own expectations for your life rather than allowing others to set them for you. This is useful in many ways that have already been mentioned, and also means that you can control how you deal with any expectations that you do set for yourself, and can choose to accept your achievements against those expectations rather than live with regret at perceived failure or with arrogance about perceived successes.

- **Be yourself.** It is of course important to be effective at your job, and it can be a pleasure to do it well. But you also need to be yourself, without compromising essential elements of your personality or principles. So, be a bit more 'you' at work, and get used to feeling comfortable with this. Tell colleagues this is what you are trying to do. If your job makes you feel you are compromising yourself too much and you cannot change the situation, you may need to look for another job, but it will be worth it.

The same thing applies in other areas of your life – be yourself, be comfortable with it and see what happens. This is an important ingredient in helping yourself to flourish.

- **Build good relationships for their own sake.** Try to build genuine human relationships in everything you do, even in a competitive arena like business where people could take advantage of you. See human beings and human relationships as an end in themselves rather than a means to another end. Be honest. I have tried this myself in business and it has the happy side-effect of actually making business better, as more people feel they can trust you and therefore want to work with you. Make it clear to others that this is your attitude towards business relationships. This does not mean that you need to be a pushover – you can operate the 'tit for tat' (or even 'tit for two tats') policy that has proved successful in game theory, the basic idea of which is that you trust people until they let you down once (or twice).

- **Exercise intellectual independence.** To overcome the variety of influences on your life, employ the same tools of intellectual independence as we discussed under 'Consumerism dominates everything', above.

- **Drive your own flourishing.** Once you have thought through who you are and what matters to you, go and give yourself the conditions you need to flourish. This is partially about 'being yourself' as noted earlier, but also about doing the things and living the life that enable you to flourish and to feel free. This may involve trying some new things or picking up the interests you once had but have forgotten about. Unplug the TV, volunteer, see friends, learn to play an instrument, join a drama group, start oil painting – whatever it is that interests you. Determine that once and for all you're going to live the life you want, and get excited about living it – use your perspective to see you only have one life so the risk is less than you might think. Having fun, being inspired and getting immersed in things ('flow') is great for us and brings more inspiration and fun in its wake.

Conclusion

This chapter has attempted to explain what we can do in our own lives to address the problems of the modern world, including steps we can take on practical matters such as getting more involved in our local community, and those we can take to help ourselves develop some of the mental tools discussed in Chapter 10. These tools aim to help us to develop greater self-determination, intellectual independence and wisdom – qualities that should enable us to experience greater choice, freedom, fulfilment and happiness in the modern world, and also in the future.

Appendix

Recommended thinking skills

Within this section are two lists providing greater detail of the specific thinking skills contained within two of the broad mental tools recommended in this book: 'Intellectual independence' and 'Abstract thinking skills'.

Intellectual independence

These skills include:

a) A questioning attitude

- A desire to question things generally, including statements from others, assumptions, what happens in the world around us and the basic assumptions that underpin our existence

- A willingness to question all the inputs one receives from the world, including from the media, books, friends, family or any other source

- An ability to understand these inputs and their sources (including any potential biases they may have) and to use this knowledge to evaluate and interpret the messages coming from them

- A desire to seek further information if one feels it is required

- An ability to find relevant and appropriate information

b) Informed decision-making

- An understanding of the issues involved in a particular decision

- Devoting attention to assessing the likely consequences of any action before taking it, weighing up options and if necessary finding further information to assist the decision-making process

c) Intellectual agility

- The ability to stand back, gain perspective and see the 'big picture' in everything one considers, in order to arrive at better-informed and considered conclusions

- The ability to switch between different levels of thinking – to reflect on both broad theoretical issues and detailed day-to-day issues, and to be able to see each in the context of the other

- The ability to draw a balanced conclusion from opposing arguments

- The awareness that there are not always perfect answers to a question and that compromise is often required

- The ability to weigh up evidence, prioritise, and be comfortable with any compromises one makes

- The ability to think and act consistently

d) A sense of self-determination and courage

- A sense that one is a self-determined, proactive creature, able to exercise some control over one's life

- An awareness that one has an impact on the world, which can be positive or negative. Also, a sense of responsibility for one's actions

- The courage to live in accordance with one's values, even if these are not consistent with the political or social norm

Abstract thinking skills

These skills include:

- Overall, learning to navigate one's way confidently around abstract thought

- Understanding what thinking is and what thoughts are

- Understanding that one can manage one's own thinking and thoughts in different ways

- Learning how particular thinking techniques (in particular, understanding the parameters and territory of a subject) can be useful, and then how to use them

- Understanding what concepts are, how they are formed, the role they play in human society and how we use them

- Understanding the concepts we most commonly use (e.g. morality) including their parameters and territory, and how to think about them.

Taking the concept of morality as an example, here are some of the factors we should consider when learning to understand it:

- Understanding it as a concept, and its parameters

- Being aware of its territory – for example, the fact that many moral issues do not have perfect solutions

- Being aware of how this affects our expectations, both for meeting the moral standards we each set ourselves, and for achieving a world that is consistent with our own values

- Being willing to consider one's attitude towards universal values, and those relating to more abstract and less immediate consequences

- Being aware of one's main moral values

- Being willing to consider how one's values should manifest themselves in one's behaviour in every aspect of life

- Regularly and honestly reviewing the consistency between one's values and one's behaviour

- Being aware that prioritization and compromise are sometimes required between different values (e.g. between maintaining individual freedom and achieving sustainability)

- Being able to make this prioritization and these compromises in a considered way and live comfortably with the consequences

- Being open-minded and reviewing one's values in the light of experience

- Managing one's attitude towards one's values so that one manages to achieve a happy balance between living comfortably with values and living in a way that is reasonably consistent with them.

References

Chapter 1

1. Mulgan, Geoff, 'The Arrival of Time Politics' in Aldrich, Tim (ed.), *About Time*, Greenleaf Publishing, Sheffield 2005, p.79.

2. Source: Eurostat 2006.

3. Kodz J. et al, 'Working Long Hours: a Review of the Evidence: Volume 1 – Main Report', DTI Employment Relations Research Series ERRS16, 2003.

4. Mulgan, Geoff, 'The Arrival of Time Politics' in Aldrich, Tim (ed.), *About Time*, Greenleaf Publishing, Sheffield 2005, p.72.

5. Lyons G. and Chatterjee K., 'A Human Perspective on the Daily Commute: Costs, Benefits and Trade-offs', UTSG 2007, p.1.

6. Hutton W. and Jones A., 'Time and Money' in Aldrich, Tim (ed.), *About Time*, Greenleaf Publishing, Sheffield 2005, p.89.

7. Hodgkinson, Tom, *How to be Idle*, Penguin Books, London 2005, p.20

8. Goodman J. and Jorgensen B., 'Time and Technology' in Aldrich, Tim (ed.), *About Time*, Greenleaf Publishing, Sheffield 2005, p.135.

9. Ibid.

10. Park A., Curtice J., Thompson K., Philips M. and Johnson M. (eds.), *British Social Attitudes: the 23rd Report: Perspectives on a Changing Society*, Sage, 2007, p.6.

11. Davies W. H., 'Leisure' in *The Nation's Favourite Poems*, BBC Books, London 1998, p.32.

Chapter 2

1. 'Saving Tranquil Places' report by CPRE, cpre.org.uk, London 2006, p.3.

2. Ibid., p.9.

3. 'Housing Supply: what is the problem?', CPRE, www.cpre.org.uk.

4. 'Green Belt: what is the problem?', CPRE, www.cpre.org.uk.

5. Barker, Kate, 'Barker Review Final Report: Recommendations', HM Treasury 2004, p.3.

6. 'Government Response to Kate Barker's Review of Housing Supply', Office of the Deputy Prime Minister, December 2005.

7. 'Saving Tranquil Places' report by CPRE, cpre.org.uk, London 2006, p.5.

8. Speech by Rt. Hon. David Miliband MP to celebrate the 80th anniversary of the

founding of the Campaign for Protection of Rural England, 'A Land Fit for the Future', London, March 9th 2007.

9. Cowell, Alan. 'Britain proposes 60 percent cuts in carbon emissions by 2050', *International Herald Tribune*, March 13th 2007.

10. Vidal, John, '10,000 Acres of Greenbelt under Threat', *The Guardian*, March 12th 2007.

11. 'World Population Prospects: 2006 Revision Highlights', United Nations, New York 2006, p.v, www.un.org/esa/population/publications/wpp2006/wpp2006_highlights.pdf.

12. CPRE Green Belt Omnibus Questions, conducted by MORI between 30 June and 4 July 2005, www.cpre.org.uk/news/view/80.

13. 'Saving Tranquil Places' report by CPRE, cpre.org.uk, London 2006, p.3.

14. 'A Countryside for Health and Well-being: The Physical and Mental Health Benefits of Green Exercise: Executive Summary', Countryside Recreation Network, 2005, p.2.

15. Thoreau, Henry David, *Walden and Civil Disobedience*, Penguin Classics, London 1996, p.131.

16. 'Engaging and Learning with the Outdoors', National Foundation for Education Research, April 2005.

17. The Rural Strategy, 2004, cited in 'Saving Tranquil Places' report by CPRE, cpre.org.uk, London 2007, p.4.

Chapter 3

1. Simms A., Oram J., MacGillivray A. and Drury J., *Ghost Town Britain*, New Economics Foundation 2002, p.14.

2. Tanya Garnett, *Wise Moves*, Transport 2000, 2003, p.35.

3. 'The Impact of Large Foodstores on Market Towns and District Centres', DETR 1998, cited in Simms A., Oram J., MacGillivray A. and Drury J., *Ghost Town Britain*, New Economics Foundation 2002, p.14.

4. Oram J., Conisbee M. and Simms A., *Ghost Town Britain 2*, New Economics Foundation 2003, p.6.

5. Ibid., p.7.

6. Michaels L. et al. 'What's Wrong With Supermarkets?' report, Corporate Watch 2004, p.19.

7. 'The Post Office Network: Government Response to Public Consultation', DTI May 2007, p.3, www.berr.gov.uk/files/file39479.pdf.

8. 'Post Offices and Community Needs in Rural and Urban Deprived Areas', ERM 2001, cited in Simms A., Oram J., MacGillivray A. and Drury J., *Ghost Town Britain*, New Economics Foundation 2002, p.20.

9. Grassroots Action on Food and Farming, www.gaff.org.uk/information.php, cited in Oram J., Conisbee M. and Simms A., *Ghost Town Britain 2*, New Economics Foundation 2003, p.7.

10. 'Supermarkets: A report on the supply of groceries from multiple stores in the UK', Competition Commission 2000, cited in 'Briefing: how to oppose a supermarket planning application', Friends of the Earth 2005, p.4.

11. Sacks, Justin, *The Money Trail*, New Economics Foundation 2002, p.115.

12. Oram J., Conisbee M. and Simms A., *Ghost Town Britain 2*, New Economics Foundation 2003, p.30.

13. Tesco Annual Review and Summary Financial Statement 2006, p.19.

14. Lawrence, Felicity, 'Former OFT chief urges inquiry into 'abuse' of market position by supermarkets', *The Guardian*, November 10th 2005.

15. Oram J., Conisbee M. and Simms A., *Ghost Town Britain 2*, New Economics Foundation 2003, p.2.

16. For results of a survey to find the UK's main 'clone towns' see Simms A., Kjell P. and Potts R., *Clone Town Britain: the survey results on the bland state of the nation*, New Economics Foundation 2005.

17. Simms A., Oram J., MacGillivray A. and Drury J., *Ghost Town Britain*, New Economics Foundation 2002, p.3.

Chapter 4

1. From Palmer, Guy, 'Briefing on the growth in one person households', Joseph Rowntree Foundation, 2006, www.jrf.org.uk/bookshop/eBooks/9781859354759.pdf.

2. Nash V. with Christie I., *Making Sense of Community*, IPPR 2003, p.17.

3. Ibid.

4. Putnam, Robert D., *Bowling Alone*, Simon & Schuster, New York 2000, p.21.

5. 'Social Capital' is defined by Putnam as 'Connections among individuals: social networks and the norms of reciprocity and trustworthiness that arise from them' in Putnam, Robert D., *Bowling Alone*, Simon & Schuster, New York 2000, p.19.

6. Putnam, Robert D., *Bowling Alone*, Simon & Schuster, New York 2000, p.21.

7. Jones E., Haenfler R. and Johnson B. with Klocke B., *The Better World Handbook*, New Society Publishers, Gabriola Island (Canada) 2001, p.136.

8. Oram J., Conisbee M. and Simms A., *Ghost Town Britain 2*, New Economics Foundation 2003, p.20.

9. Hamilton, Clive, *Growth Fetish*, Pluto Press, London 2004, p.42.

10. 'Independent Lives Lead to Loneliness', WRVS 2004, cited in Hickman, Leo, *A Good Life*, Eden Project Books, London 2005, p.234.

11. Jones E., Haenfler R. and Johnson B. with Klocke B., *The Better World Handbook*, New Society Publishers, Gabriola Island (Canada) 2001, p.136.

12. Putnam, Robert D., *Bowling Alone*, Simon & Schuster, New York 2000, p.326.

13. Ibid., p.283.

14. Oram J., Conisbee M. and Simms A., *Ghost Town Britain 2*, New Economics Foundation 2003, p.20.

15. Putnam, Robert D., *Bowling Alone*, Simon & Schuster, New York 2000, p.326.

16. From 'The Communications Market 2007: Nations and Regions', Ofcom, p.102, www.ofcom.org.uk/research/cm/cm07/uk/uk3.pdf.

17. Putnam, Robert D., *Bowling Alone*, Simon & Schuster, New York 2000, p.326.

Chapter 5

1. 'Planning for Consumer Change', Henley Centre, 2004. Rather sweetly, the report in which this figure was originally found (from an advertising agency called PPA Marketing, entitled 'Communication Uncovered', p.4) also notes that 'as a consequence of this massive number of commercial messages people are beginning to find this constant bombardment annoying'.

2. Thursday December 21st 2006.

3. 'A Product Placement Hall of Fame', *Business Week Online* 1998, www.businessweek.com/1998/25/b3583062.htm.

4. Klein, Naomi, *No Logo*, Flamingo, London 2000, p.80.

5. Teather, David, 'Has Coke become the new McDonald's?', *Guardian Unlimited*, August 18th 2006.

6. Williams, Zoe. 'Commercialisation of Childhood', report for Compass, www.compassonline.org.uk, 2006, p.11.

7. Boyle, David, *Authenticity*, Harper Perennial, London 2004, p.7 of 'Meet the Author' section.

8. Reeves, Richard, 'The Politics of Happiness', NEF Discussion paper, www.neweconomics.org, 2003, p.7.

9. Ibid., p.5.

10. Ibid., p.8.

11. Ibid., p.8.

Chapter 6

1. Keaney E. and Rogers B., 'A Citizen's Duty: Voter inequality and the case for compulsory turnout', IPPR, May 2006, p.10.

2. 'Audit of Political Engagement 4', The Hansard Society and The Electoral Commission, 2006, p.11.

3. Ibid.

4. Weir S., Margetts H. and Ross M., 'State of the Nation', Joseph Rowntree Reform Trust 2004, cited in 'Power to the People: Final Report', The Power Inquiry 2006, p.77.

5. Keaney E. and Rogers B., 'A Citizen's Duty: Voter inequality and the case for compulsory turnout', IPPR, May 2006, p.13.

6. 'Audit of Political Engagement 4', The Hansard Society and The Electoral Commission, 2006, p.6

7. 'Power to the People: Final Report', The Power Inquiry 2006, p.42.

8. Ibid., p.43.

9. Ibid., p.43.

10. Ibid., p.42.

11. Keaney E. and Rogers B., 'A Citizen's Duty: Voter inequality and the case for compulsory turnout', IPPR, May 2006, p.9.

12. 'Power to the People: Final Report', The Power Inquiry 2006, p.66.

13. Ibid., p.64.

14. Stanley, Timothy, 'Gordon Brown Take Note', *Guardian Unlimited,* July 4th 2006, http://politics.guardian.co.uk/comment/story/0,,1811814,00.html.

15. Sanders et al., 'The 2005 General Election in Great Britain Report for The Electoral Commission', Electoral Commission, cited in Keaney E. and Rogers B., 'A Citizen's Duty: Voter inequality and the case for compulsory turnout', IPPR, May 2006, p.16.

16. Non-Voters Survey (May 7th-15th 2005), Power Inquiry, cited in 'Power to the People: Final Report', The Power Inquiry 2006, p.93.

17. 'Power to the People: Final Report', The Power Inquiry 2006, p.120.

18. Keaney E. and Rogers B., 'A Citizen's Duty: Voter inequality and the case for compulsory turnout', IPPR, May 2006, p.11.

19. Ibid., p.5.

Chapter 7

1. www.intel.com/technology/mooreslaw.

2. www.pandia.com/sew/383-web-size.html.

3. Direct Mail Information Service, www.dmis.com.

4. Hughes J. and Thomas P., 'BLT: The Big Lifestyle Trade-Off', *The Ecologist*, 2006, www.theecologist.org/archive_detail.asp?content_id=622.

5. Giddens, Anthony, *The Third Way: the renewal of social democracy*, Polity Press, Cambridge 1998, p.109.

Chapter 8

1. Another large group exists in the modern Western world, however, that is not lucky enough to have these opportunities. Yet this group is still sold the same expectations as the more privileged group, perhaps making the effect of these expectations even more damaging for this non-privileged group.

Chapter 9

1. Shah H. and McIvor M., *A New Political Economy: Compass Programme for Renewal*, Lawrence and Wishart, London 2006, p.23.

2. The broader costs – for example the effect of air freight on the environment – are rarely factored in to this process.

3. Hamilton, Clive, *Growth Fetish*, Pluto Press, London 2004, p.122.

4. 'The World at Six Billion: Part 1', United Nations, New York 1999, p.3, http://www.un.org/esa/population/publications/sixbillion/sixbilpart1.pdf.

5. 'World Population Prospects: 2006 Revision Highlights', United Nations, New York 2006, p.v, www.un.org/esa/population/publications/wpp2006/wpp2006_highlights.pdf.

6. Reeves, Richard, 'The Politics of Happiness', NEF discussion paper, New Economics Foundation 2003, p.6.

7. Hamilton, Clive, *Growth Fetish*, Pluto Press, London 2004, pp.28-9.

8. Ibid., p.209.

9. Shah H. and McIvor M., *A New Political Economy: Compass Programme for Renewal*, Lawrence and Wishart, London 2006, p.24.

10. Ibid., p.24.

11. Ibid., p.24.

12. Porritt, Jonathon, *Capitalism as if the World Matters*, Earthscan, London 2006, p.111.

13. Mill, John Stuart, *Principles of Political Economy*, Oxford World's Classics, Oxford 1998, p.124.

14. Ibid., p.126.

15. This is aside from the fact that the current version of the free market is actually not free in any sense of the word, but deliberately biased towards the wealthy – for example in the form of the Common Agricultural Policy that pays farming subsidies to European nations.

16. *Our Common Future*, World Commission on Environment and Development, OUP, Oxford 1987.

17. Porritt, Jonathon, *Capitalism as if the World Matters*, Earthscan, London 2006, p.22.

18. Although it should be acknowledged that throughout the ages there have been commentators and thinkers arguing for an increase in the intellectual armoury of human beings.

19. Woodward D. and Simms A., *Growth Isn't Working*, New Economics Foundation 2006, p.1.

20. From Oxfam UK Poverty Programme, www.oxfamgb.org/ukpp/poverty/thefacts.htm.

21. This line differs for each country and is calculated as those with below 60% of contemporary net median disposable income in 2000/01. From Oxfam UK Poverty Programme, www.oxfamgb.org/ukpp/poverty/thefacts.htm.

22. Hamilton, Clive, *Growth Fetish*, Pluto Press, London 2004, p.144.

23. From Keaney E. and Rogers B., 'A Citizen's Duty: Voter inequality and the case for compulsory turnout', IPPR, May 2006, p.12.

24. Woodward D. and Simms A., *Growth Isn't Working*, New Economics Foundation 2006, p.3.

25. Ibid., p.3.

26. 'Ecological Footprint and Biocapacity 2006 Edition', Global Footprint Network, www.footprintnetwork.org/download.php?id=305.

27. From Global Footprint Network, www.footprintnetwork.org/gfn_sub.php?content=global_footprint

28. Porritt, Jonathon, *Capitalism as if the World Matters*, Earthscan, London 2006, p.60.

29. From www.wwf.org.uk.

30. 'Climate Change 2007: Impacts, Adaptation and Vulnerability', Working Group II contribution to IPCC Fourth Assessment report, Intergovernmental Panel on Climate Change 2007, p.5, http://www.ipcc.ch/SPM13apr07.pdf.

31. Ibid.

32. Porritt, Jonathon, *Capitalism as if the World Matters*, Earthscan, London 2006, p.84.

33. 'Examples of Unfair Trade Rules', World Development Movement website, www.wdm.org.uk/campaigns/trade/indepth/unfairtraderules.htm.

34. One consequence of this is the popularity of the view that new technology alone will get us out of our environmental problems. Whilst technology can clearly play an important role in this process, the idea that it is the panacea for these problems is absurd as it fails to recognise that consumption cannot rise forever as there are basic limits on the natural resources we have available, and ultimately our consumption depends on these resources.

Chapter 10

1. NEF Introduction paper, 2006, p.1.

2. Another way to portray this is as regulation to ensure that important freedoms are not threatened.

3. Shah H. and Marks N., *A Well-Being Manifesto for a Flourishing Society*, New Economics Foundation, London 2004, p.7.

4. Porritt, Jonathon, *Capitalism as if the World Matters*, Earthscan, London 2006, p.102.

5. Hamilton, Clive, *Growth Fetish*, Pluto Press, London 2004, p.222.

6. Shah H. and Marks N., *A Well-Being Manifesto for a Flourishing Society*, New Economics Foundation, London 2004, p.8.

7. Porritt, Jonathon, *Capitalism as if the World Matters*, Earthscan, London 2006, p.226.

8. Shah H. and Marks N., *A Well-Being Manifesto for a Flourishing Society*, New Economics Foundation, London 2004, p.8.

9. Ibid., p.10.

10. From Ibid., p.9.

11. These recommendations are taken from Oram J., Conisbee M. and Simms A., *Ghost Town Britain 2*, New Economics Foundation 2003.

12. For more information, see Oram J., Conisbee M. and Simms A., *Ghost Town Britain 2*, New Economics Foundation 2003.

13. 'Power to the People: Final Report', The Power Inquiry 2006, p.24.

14. Some of these recommendations are taken from 'Power to the People: Final Report', The Power Inquiry 2006.

15. For more discussion of this topic, see Docwra, Richard, 'Mental Slavery – Edit', www.changestar.co.uk/thinking_papers.htm.

16. Reeves, Richard. 'The Politics of Happiness', NEF Discussion paper, www.neweconomics.org, 2003, p.22.

17. Shah H. and Marks N., *A Well-Being Manifesto for a Flourishing Society*, New Economics Foundation, London 2004, p.12.

18. A comparable idea is getting involved in a game in a committed way, whilst realising it is ultimately just a game and remembering to enjoy it.

19. Forum for the Future 2005, cited in Porritt, Jonathon, *Capitalism as if the World Matters*, Earthscan, London 2006, pp.294-5.

Chapter 11

1. This suggestion comes from Jones E., Haenfler R. and Johnson B. with Klocke B., *The Better World Handbook*, New Society Publishers, Canada 2001, p.138.

Further reading and links

I have provided below a list of a few books and resources that you could use to find out more about the issues raised in the book and to take things further should you want to. They represent just the tip of the iceberg of the resources and organisations actually available, but they should provide a reasonable 'way in' to these issues.

Do have a look at the books, reports and links listed in the references for each chapter too – many of these are well worth examining in more detail.

Books

Aldrich, Tim (ed.). *About Time*, Greenleaf Publishing, Sheffield, 2005.

Boyle, David. *Authenticity*, Harper Perennial, London, 2004.

Edwards, David. *Free to be Human*, Green Books, Dartington, 2000.

Hamilton, Clive. *Growth Fetish*, Pluto Press, London, 2004.

Hickman, Leo. *A Good Life*, Eden Project Books, London, 2005.

Hodgkinson, Tom. *How to be Idle*, Penguin Books, London, 2005.

Honoré, Carl. *In Praise of Slow*, Orion Books, London, 2005.

Jones E., Haenfler R. and Johnson B. with Klocke B. *The Better World Handbook*, New Society Publishers, Canada, 2001.

Klein, Naomi. *No Logo*, Flamingo, London, 2000.

LaFollette, Hugh (ed.). *The Blackwell Guide to Ethical Theory*, Blackwell, Oxford, 2003.

Mill, John Stuart. *Principles of Political Economy*, Oxford World's Classics, Oxford, 1998.

Nozick, Robert. *Anarchy, State and Utopia*, Blackwell, Oxford, 2003.

Porritt, Jonathon. *Capitalism as if the World Matters*, Earthscan, London, 2006.

Putnam, Robert D. *Bowling Alone*, Simon & Schuster, New York, 2000.

Rawls, John. *A Theory of Justice*, Oxford University Press, Oxford, 1999.

Russell, Bertrand. *The Conquest of Happiness*, George Allen & Unwin, London, 1943.

Schumacher, E.F. *Small is Beautiful*, Sphere Books, London, 1987.

Thoreau, Henry David. *Walden and Civil Disobedience*, Penguin Classics, London, 1996.

Wolff, Jonathan. *An Introduction to Political Philosophy*, Oxford University Press, Oxford, 1996.

Magazines

Prospect – www.prospect-magazine.co.uk
Resurgence – www.resurgence.org
The Ecologist – www.theecologist.org/home.asp

Links

The Big Picture: politics, economics, social justice and sustainability

ChangeStar, www.changestar.co.uk
Compass, www.compassonline.org.uk
FEASTA, www.feasta.org
Forum for the Future, www.forumforthefuture.org.uk
New Economics Foundation, www.neweconomics.org
Schumacher UK, www.schumacher.org.uk
The Simultaneous Policy, www.simpol.org
World Future Council, www.worldfuturecouncil.org
Worldwatch Institute, www.worldwatch.org

Campaigning and ideas for action on individual issues

General

Anti Apathy, www.antiapathy.org
Center for a New American Dream, www.newdream.org
Ethical Junction, www.ethical-junction.org
Friends of the Earth, www.foe.co.uk
Global Action Plan, www.globalactionplan.org.uk
London Sustainability Exchange, www.lsx.org.uk
Media Lens, www.medialens.org
OneWorld.net, www.oneworld.net
OpenDemocracy, www.opendemocracy.net
Oxfam, www.oxfam.org.uk
People and Planet, www.peopleandplanet.org
The New Road Map Foundation, www.newroadmap.org
We Are What We Do, www.wearewhatwedo.org
World Development Movement, www.wdm.org.uk
Worldwide Fund for Nature, www.wwf.org

Our lives are too rushed

Anxiety Culture, www.anxietyculture.com
The Idler, www.idler.co.uk
The Long Now Foundation, www.longnow.org
Slow Food, www.slowfood.com

Our natural spaces are under threat

Campaign to Protect Rural England, www.cpre.org.uk
Natural England, www.naturalengland.org.uk
The Wildlife Trusts, www.wildlifetrusts.org

Shopping is hell

Certified Farmers Markets, www.farmersmarkets.net
Corporate Watch, www.corporatewatch.org.uk
CorpWatch, www.corpwatch.org
LETS Link, www.letslinkuk.net
Scottish Farmers Markets, www.scottishfarmersmarkets.co.uk

We're losing our communities

Community Action Network, www.can-online.org.uk
Community Service Volunteers, www.csv.org.uk
Do-It, www.do-it.org.uk
Fair Shares, www.fairshares.org.uk
Green Drinks, www.greendrinks.org
'Local/Green Socials', www.changestar.co.uk/initiatives2.htm
TimeBank, www.timebank.org.uk
Transition Towns, www.transitiontowns.org
TV-Turnoff Network, www.tvturnoff.org
White Dot, www.whitedot.org

Consumerism dominates everything

Adbusters, www.adbusters.org

We're not involved in politics

Have Your Say, www.haveyoursayonline.net
MySociety, www.mysociety.org
Our World Our Say, www.owos.info
The Power Inquiry, www.makeitanissue.org.uk

Index

Note: page references in **Bold** indicate
entire chapters